THIS AIN'T NO PICNIC

YOUR PUNK ROCK VEGAN COOKBOOK

JOSHUA PLOEG
WITH PHOTOGRAPHY BY
VICE COOLER &
DALTON BLANCO

THIS AIN'T NO PICNIC
YOUR PUNK ROCK VEGAN COOKBOOK

Joshua Ploeg

First Printing, April 1, 2014
ISBN 9780977055753
This is Microcosm #76124

Photography by Vice Cooler + Dalton Blanco
Cover design by Joe Biel
Illustrated and Designed by Meggyn Pomerleau

Printed on post-consumer paper in the U.S.

Distributed by IPG, Chicago and Turnaround, UK

Microcosm Publishing
2752 N Williams St.
Portland, OR 97227
www.microcosmpublishing.com

Thanks to The Minutemen for inspiring *so* much deliciousness.

THIS AIN'T NO PICNIC

YOUR PUNK ROCK VEGAN COOKBOOK

JOSHUA PLOEG

with photography by
VICE COOLER & DALTON BLANCO

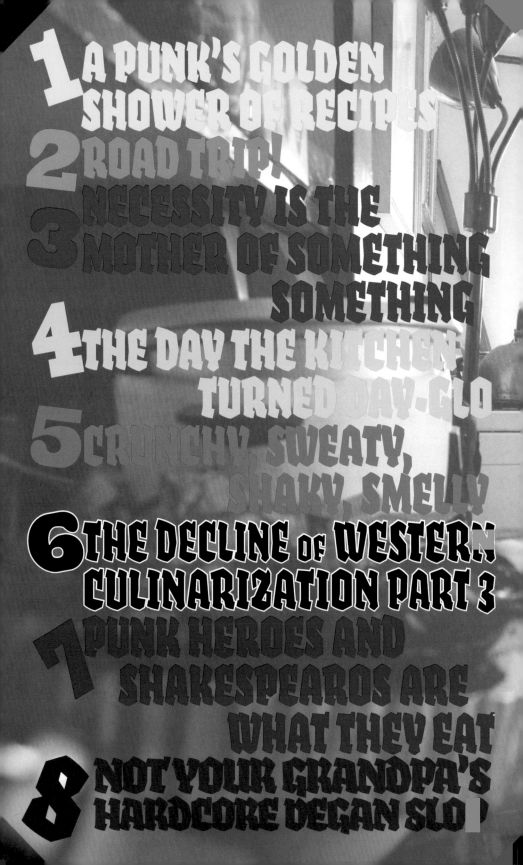

TABLE OF CONTENTS

RECIPES

After all of these years, even though some people call me *"the punk rock vegan chef"* because I tour with food and still do buffets and demos at shows, at one point did a live cooking show with a backing band, and everything is still overly DIY and sketchy much of the time, I've still never done a punk-themed cookbook or zine. So we thought it would be fun to give it a whirl. Of course merely having recipes was not going to be enough, so we thought it would be entertaining to have photos. But, of course, if they were just of food that would be pretty passe, so people and their finery, dogs, and mess must also be included. Some of it must have little to do with anything.

A mish mash of random quotes, playlists, and intros by various people from my life that range from zany to academic also needed to be included. There needed to be some interesting tips and methods for cooking without basic needs. This represents the circumstances that can come about from a series of bad choices. But that's one nice thing about punk and other DIY "cultures"—winding up in a tough spot at the end of the day doesn't stop you from having a good time, sustaining yourself, or being able to do what you need to do...one way or another.

So voila, this tome came to be.

You may wonder why there isn't also a picture for this and that, or why there is one of something else, or why this or that person isn't in here..well live my life and you would know the answer—Haha! Seriously, what part of "on no budget," "when I say I'll get that to you in a week I actually mean never," or "what's scheduling?" don't you understand?! It's shocking we managed to accomplish this much! In an attempt to keep it real, some mistakes are catalogued. Life ain't pretty, punk ain't pretty, and food ain't always pretty either. Neither are crusties.

Punk means different things to different people, with the general rule being that you can recognize a punk because they love to argue about it, subcompartmentalize, and judge non-judiciously. That's nice, have fun in your mom's basement. Reminds me of when Varg Vikernes killed Euronymous. We're better than that—so stop being such a hesher about it!

As someone who entered punk culture after punk was already dead...it tends to take on a life of its own, and you get the chance to tailor it to your own needs and circle of friends. That's some versatile shit, and it also becomes personal. That's probably why so many people are uptight about it. Oh well, I'm pretty over it—I play hardcore, go to and put on shows, cook and tour DIY and still live in warehouses and dirty-ass punk houses where bands practice so if you don't dig what I'm laying down here, mosey on. Or in the immortal words of Brett Frost "fuck you if you doubt me!"

Particular interests, like crusties, that I find amusing: using what's in the cupboard, making something out of nothing, tongue-in-cheekly paying tribute to "idols" (which of course we're not supposed to have—yet there are college courses and whole books on these people!?), smashing tradition, ushering in half-baked concepts and fully-formed manifestations of crazy ideas—that's what punk-themed cookbooks are made of, or at least this one.

It is what it is, enjoy it for that, rather than what it ain't. I know that's a tall order in this day and age, but similarly to my life, this book is meant to be random, kinda fun and moderately useful. So try to have some fun, okay? With its confluence of fashion, design, music, food, and concept, it's like you have a crappy little gallery opening right here in your hand. So please sit back with a few hors d'ouvres and a 40 oz. and enjoy the party!

much love,

Joshua Ploeg

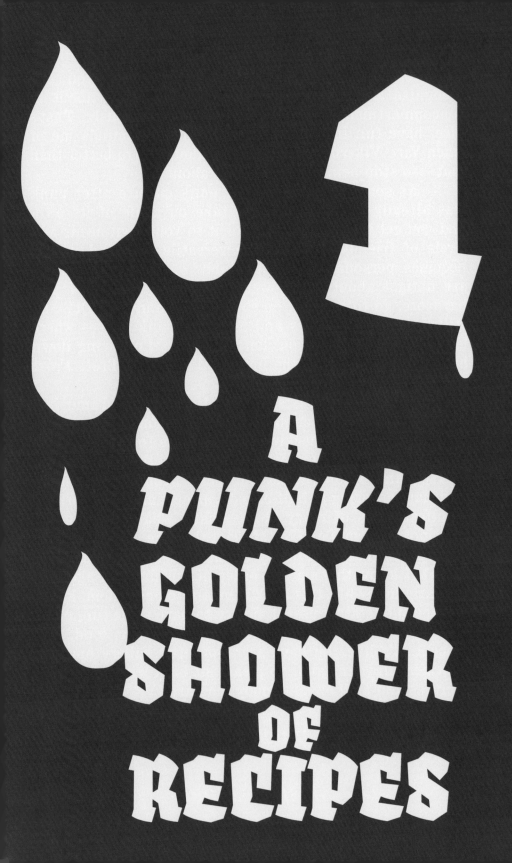

1

A PUNK'S GOLDEN SHOWER OF RECIPES

Every punk loves to either collect records or at least a vast, smarmy knowledge, or pretend knowledge, of said records. Punks love food, they are always hungry, starving if you will. Many songs are odes to the morsels that we crave after playing a show or pogoing like the dickens all night. Late night and fast food fare rule the school of songs that mention edibles. We thought it would be fun to make recipes out of a good sampling of some of these delicious tunes, so you can add them to your collection. So here are the various foods mentioned in punk rock songs and titles, brought to life for your enjoyment!

Punk's Golden Shower of Recipes
by Zack Carlson

Like drugs, love, and other unhealthy obsessions, gastronomic fixations can lead to unexpected inspiration. Years before Weird Al Yankovic forged a career singing about Twinkies and ice cream, punk and new wave acts raised the banner of junk food anthems.

See, different types of humans require different types of food. While the hoity-toity upper-crusters were nibbling Beluga caviar at the country club, punks were emptying their threadbare pockets to grab a slice of pizza pie, or making a three-course meal out of Pringles® , jerky, and Twizzlers®. The lower class has a palate too, ya' know, and we're never gonna rest until we see it *satisfied.*

Shriekers and guitar-manglers have long been powered by the raging storm in their bellies, ready to lash out at the world that keeps them hungry. From The Dickies "Shake and Bake" recipe to Fear's mouth-watering "Beef! Beef! Beef!... Beef Balogna!!," punk and food have stayed intertwined.

Sadly, the relationship could also be abusive. For every track that celebrated the delights of the kitchen, there was a digestive ode from a darker, more questionable place. For example, see Angry Samoans' "Tuna Taco." *Or don't.*

But through all the burger damage and sugar rage we've endured through the decades, one thing has remained consistent: *Punks gotta eat.* And if we can't get our hands on the following recipes, we can always eat the rich.

Here's a bunch of songs for the playlist—
All food all the time!

1 – THE VANDALS "ANARCHYBURGER"
2 – X-RAY SPEX "JUNK FOOD JUNKIE"
3 – RAMONES "I JUST WANNA HAVE SOMETHING TO DO"
4 – 1.6 BAND "BEEF STEW"
5 – DESCENDENTS "WIENERSCHNITZEL"
6 – MDC "CORPORATE DEATH BURGER"
(Yet again the burger becomes some metaphor in the battle of freedom v. oppression.)
7 – THE BAGS "GLUTTONY"
8 – BORN AGAINST "WELL FED FUCK" *(Yes indeed.)*
9 – SHONEN KNIFE "BROWN MUSHROOMS"
10 – DROPDEAD "UNJUSTIFIED MURDER"
11 – SIOUXSIE AND THE BANSHEES "HONG KONG GARDEN"
12 – RAIN LIKE THE SOUND OF TRAINS "COOKING WITH ANGER" *(The only way to cook— haha! Actually, you've got to be mellow in my kitchen.)*
13 – ALL "ALFREDO'S"
14 – BLEED "WHITE CRUST NO BREAD"
15 – LUNACHICKS "MMM DONUTS"
16 – TOTAL COELO "I EAT CANNIBAL"
(This is important to know about even though it's definitely not a punk rock song by any stretch.)
17 – DOGGY STYLE "DONUT SHOP ROCK"
18 – GANG OF FOUR "CHEESEBURGER"
19 – FEAR "BEEF BALONEY"
20 – THE CLASH "LOST IN THE SUPERMARKET" *(I know the feeling.)*
21 – SPLODGENOUSSABOUNDS "TWO PINTS OF LAGER AND A PACKET OF CRISPS" *(Or maybe just the crisps.)*

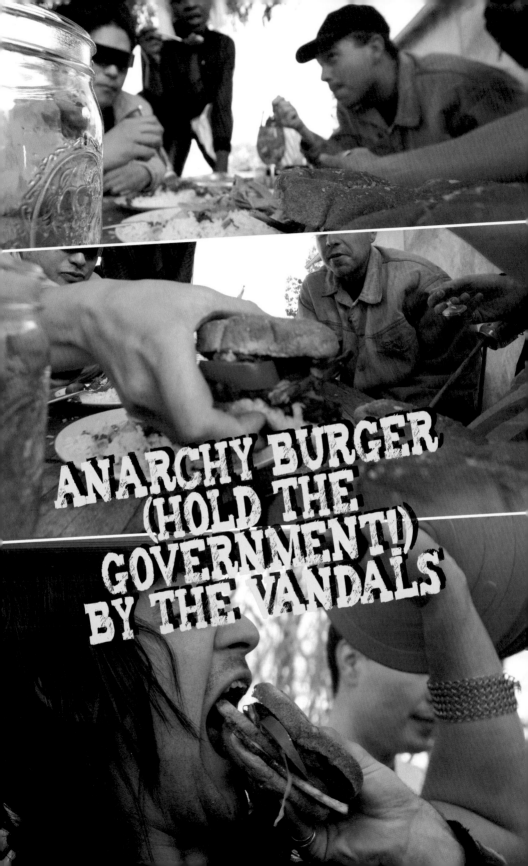

-PATTY-

1 C. COOKED LENTILS
1 C. BEETS, MINCED IN A FOOD PROCESSOR
1/4 TO 1/2 C. TAPIOCA OR POTATO STARCH
TAMARI, SALT, AND PEPPER, CUMIN, AND ANY OTHER
SPICES TO TASTE
2 GARLIC CLOVES, MINCED
1/4 C. MINCED ONION

-FRENCH FRIES-

1 OR 2 POTATOES
SALT TO TASTE
OIL FOR COATING

-SAUTÉED TOPPING-

1/2 C. CHOPPED BELL PEPPER
1/2 C. SLICED MUSHROOMS
1 OR 2 MINCED HOT PEPPERS
1/2 C. *(or more!)* SLICED ONIONS
2-4 MINCED GARLIC CLOVES
SMALL AMOUNT OF OIL FOR SAUTÉ
SALT AND PEPPER TO TASTE
some herbs are nice, like **DILL OR OREGANO**

-QUICK CHILI-

1 C. COOKED LENTILS
1/4 C. BARBEQUE SAUCE
2 OR 3 TSP. CHILI SAUCE
CUMIN, CORIANDER, PAPRIKA, CHILI POWDER, SALT,
AND BLACK PEPPER TO TASTE
2 TSP. MINCED PICKLES
1/4 C. CHOPPED ONIONS

-ANIMAL SAUCE-

1 TSP. OIL
1 TSP. LEMON JUICE
1 GARLIC CLOVE
1 TSP. TOMATO PASTE
1 TSP. GRATED ONION
1/2 TSP. MUSTARD POWDER
2 TSP. PICKLES
1/4 C. TOFU, COOKED WHITE BEANS, OR
COCONUT MILK/CREAM
1 TSP. PREPARED HORSERADISH *(I like it, anyway)*
WHITE PEPPER, SALT, AND SUGAR TO TASTE
1/4 C. SOYMILK, CASHEW MILK *or whatever (unsweetened***)**

SAUERKRAUT
TOASTED BUNS

NOT: meat, that's the government!!

(I was thinking the government was the bun, but that sounds depressing, however you can declare the bun is in fact the government and leave it out if you wish) Lettuce may also be the government or possibly a narc, so I left that out as well.

Mix the **PATTY** ingredients together, add more starch/flour if you want or need to in order to make them malleable with your hands. Season to taste. Make into balls and flatten in a heated skillet with light oil. Flatten with a spatula and cook, turning once until nice and browned on both sides.

It is fairly easy to make **FRENCH FRIES** in the oven. Cut potatoes into strips of your desired size. Coat with salt and oil and bake on a cooking sheet at 450, turning once, for 20-30 minutes or until crispy but not burnt, of course. Keep an eye on them.

Cook the **SAUTÉ** ingredients in a small amount of oil until done to your liking *(I enjoy slightly blackened onions personally).* In order to achieve varied degrees of cookedness, obviously you can add the veggies to the pan at different times. Salt and pepper to taste.

Mix the **QUICK CHILI** ingredients and cook for five minutes. Adjust seasonings *(sounds familiar).*

And of course lastly, blend the **ANIMAL SAUCE** ingredients together to taste. And you can fry your sauerkraut as well, if you like. Compose everything. Your bun goes on the outside. *Maybe.*

"I LIKE FOOD BETTER THAN I LIKE PUNK ROCK BUT IT WASN'T ALWAYS THAT WAY"
- MATTY LANDLINE (SERENGHETTO)

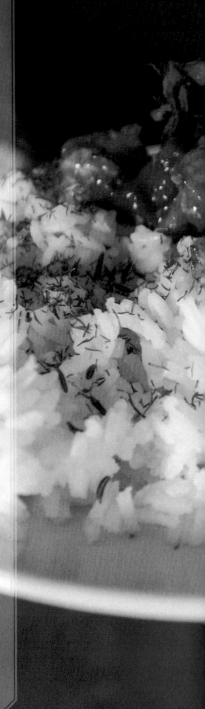

-VINDALOO PASTE-

1 TSP. CUMIN SEED
1/2 TSP. CARDAMOM SEEDS
CINNAMON STICK, AN INCH
OR TWO
1/4 TSP. CLOVES
1/2 TSP. BLACK MUSTARD
SEED
1/2 TSP. FENUGREEK
1 TSP. CHILI POWDER
1/2 TSP. SALT
2 DRIED HOT CHILIES
1 BAY LEAF
1 TSP. VINEGAR
1 TSP. LEMON JUICE
2 TSP. GRATED ONION
1/4 C. WATER *(more if necessary)*
2 TSP. OIL

-VINDALOO-

1 LB. VEGAN "CHICKN,"
CHOPPED *(if you don't like fake meat,
use tofu, mushrooms, or eggplant—durrrrr!)*
1 OR 2 DICED POTATOES
1 ONION, CHOPPED
3 GARLIC CLOVES, MINCED
2 TSP. GINGER, MINCED
1 TSP. TURMERIC, GROUND
1 TSP. CORIANDER BERRIES,
CRUSHED
1 FRESH HOT PEPPER,
MINCED
1 RED BELL PEPPER,
MINCED
1 C. TOMATO SAUCE
1 OR 2 TSP. TAMARIND
PASTE
1/4 C. BROWN SUGAR
(omit if you don't give a shit)
LEMON JUICE TO TASTE
SALT AND PEPPER TO
TASTE
A FEW TSP. OLIVE OIL
HOT SAUCE TO TASTE

CHICKN VINDALOO (RAMONES "I JUST WANNA HAVE SOMETHING TO DO")

This is the most useful and pleasing of their culinary lyrical moments. I've made this complicated, but that's because they are deeper than they ever got credit for. Plus, *this is my jam!*

Toast the dry ingredients for the **VINDALOO PASTE** briefly in a dry pan. Grind them until fine. Mix with the other ingredients to form a paste. Set aside.

Fry the potatoes for the **VINDALOO** with salt and pepper in some olive oil until browned. Set aside. Fry the onions, ginger, and garlic briefly in olive oil. Add vegan chickn, salt and pepper to taste, turmeric, coriander, and fry until browned. Add minced peppers and vindaloo paste and stir, cooking for a few minutes. Add the potatoes.

Mix brown sugar, tamarind, and lemon juice into the tomato sauce and add this to the pan. Cook for 10-15 minutes, adding water or broth to thin it out if necessary, and additional hot sauce or salt to taste. Serve with rice.

WIENERSCHNITZEL (DESCENDENTS)

Let's make this interesting. It really would be a breaded veal cutlet, but who cares?! Mushroom flour is an intriguing substance you can add to a lot of things to improve taste and texture. As you may have guessed, you should be listening to these songs when you make the recipes. Zany fun.

**1/2 C. DRIED MUSHROOMS
1 LB. TOFU
1/3 C. TAPIOCA FLOUR
2 MINCED GARLIC CLOVES
1 OR 2 TSP. TAMARI OR AMINOS OR SOME SUCH
1 TSP. ONION POWDER
1/2 C. MINCED PARSLEY
1 C. BREADCRUMBS
SEVERAL TSP. LEMON JUICE
1 TSP. MUSTARD
OIL FOR FRYING AND DREDGING, NOT A LOT
A LITTLE FLOUR OR POTATO FLOUR OR OTHER
SALT AND PEPPER TO TASTE**

Okay! Grind up those dried mushrooms into mostly a powder. Next, mix with the tofu, garlic, tapioca flour, tamari, a little oil, onion powder, half of the parsley, and salt and pepper to taste. Form into flat patties, adding more flour if needed. Mix mustard, lemon juice, and a little oil together. Set aside. Separately toss remaining parsley, breadcrumbs, and salt and pepper together to taste with a little extra flour or potato flour or your choice. Dredge patties in mustard-lemon juice mixture then in breadcrumbs and fry in a little oil (or bake at 400) turning once, until browned on both sides. Serve with scallions and gravy, or cooked apples, coleslaw, potatoes... that sort of thing. Or on a bun, that's great too!

POT ROAST
("GLUTTONY" BY ALICE BAG BAND)

Alice Bag is cool, still playing music and doing book tours and representin'. And of course, this song is one of the fun highlights of *Decline*... pay no mind to the salivating brrrooooood!! There's no law that says everything has to be fake meat right? I'm pretty sick of it too, I know I know...so why not a different sort of "pot roast." I swear you can be gluttonous with this one as well. Pork out!

1 PUMPKIN
1 ONION, PEELED AND CUT INTO LARGE CHUNKS
3 OR 4 SPRIGS ROSEMARY
1 HEAD GARLIC, SEPARATED INTO CLOVES BUT NOT PEELED
2 OR 3 BEETS, TRIMMED AND CUT INTO WEDGES
12 ASPARAGUS SPEARS, TRIMMED
SEA SALT TO TASTE
SEVERAL TBSP. OLIVE OIL
SEVERAL TBSP. BROTH
1 TSP. SMOKED PAPRIKA

Cut pumpkin in half and take the seeds and goop out *(actually, give the bugger a good wash too)*. Place in a large baking dish or Dutch oven and score the flesh deeply. Sprinkle with some broth, olive oil, salt, and pepper. Bake at 350 for 20 minutes. Add everything else except asparagus, including additional broth and paprika, and season to taste. Bake for 25 more, basting occasionally in its own juices. Like a capitalist. Add asparagus and continue cooking for 15-20 minutes. Serve in sizeable chunks with the roasted vegetables and some garlic mashed potatoes.

SHONEN KNIFE "BROWN MUSHROOMS"

Yes, I know they're talking about *that* kind of mushroom, but we're modifying here. Don't trip.

2 C. SLICED SHIITAKES
1/2 C. DICED ONION
2 MINCED GARLIC CLOVES
1-2 TSP. TAMARI
1/4 C. SESAME SEEDS
1 TSP. AGAVE
2 TSP. BLACK BEAN OR SOYBEAN SAUCE
OIL FOR SAUTÉ
2 TSP. RICE FLOUR
BLACK PEPPER AND SALT TO TASTE
1/2 TSP. FIVE-SPICE

Coat mushrooms in half of the tamari and agave, and a little oil. Mix sesame seeds, five-spice, rice flour, and salt to taste and coat the mushrooms with this. Coat a pan with oil and heat to med-high and begin frying mushrooms. Cook for two minutes, turn, add garlic and onions. Continue cooking for several minutes till crispy. I like a pretty good coating of sesame seeds on these. Just before they are done, mix the rest of the tamari and agave with bean sauce and a little water *(mustard too if you like)*, and pour it over the mushrooms. Remove it from the heat and serve with rice.

CHOP SUEY
(SIOUXSIE AND THE BANSHEES "HONG KONG GARDEN")

British new wavers and punks were for a time obsessed with the "orient." And there was that connection of punk shows at chinese restaurants like Cathay DeGrande and Mabuhay Garden. This song has some pretty questionable lyrics, and chop suey is *terrible*. But here we are, making it delicious. All of it. Plus, who doesn't love Siouxsie?!

1 C. SLICED BOK CHOY
1/2 C. CHOPPED CELERY
1/2 C. SLICED OR DICED ONIONS
1/2 C. DICED CARROTS
1/3 C. MUNG BEAN SPROUTS
1/2 C. CHOPPED BELL PEPPER
1/2 C. CHOPPED ROASTED PEANUTS
3 MINCED GARLIC CLOVES
1 TSP. TAMARI
1 TSP. MUSTARD
1 TSP. HOISIN OR PLUM SAUCE
1 TSP. CHILI SAUCE OR 1 MINCED CHILI PEPPER
1 TSP. SESAME SEEDS
1 TSP. TOASTED SESAME OIL
OIL FOR FRYING/SAUTÉ
WONTON WRAPPERS, CUT INTO STRIPS
SALT AND PEPPER TO TASTE
2 SCALLIONS, MINCED

Begin by frying onions, garlic, and peppers with a tad of salt and pepper for two minutes in a little oil. Add the rest of the veggies *(reserving some sprouts and the scallions)* and sesame oil, and sauté for another minute or two. Add the tamari, mustard, hoisin, chili, peanuts, and half of the scallions, and cook for a few minutes more. Season to taste.

Somewhere in this train of events, fry the won ton strips in some oil until crispy. Salt them modestly and allow to drain on absorbent paper.

Serve your lovely chop suey with rice or noodles, garnish with the rest of the mung bean sprouts, scallions, and wonton strips. Of course you could add snow peas, bamboo, water chestnut, tofu or whatever else to the cooking if you like. Five Spice Tofu is a fine addition!

Those SoCal boys love their takeout. I've rendered this in an amusing fashion, making it as inauthentic as possible.

MASSIVE ENCHILADAS WITH RICE AND BEANS (A LA "ALFREDO'S")

LARGE CORN TORTILLAS
(not the easiest thing in the world to find, but get the biggest ones you can)

2 HEADS SPINACH
2 C. TOMATILLOS
1 LB. TOFU
2 C. DICED ONIONS
3-4 GARLIC CLOVES
LIME JUICE
1 TSP. EACH CORIANDER, CUMIN, CHILI POWDER
1/2 C. CHOPPED CILANTRO
1 C. DICED GREEN BELL PEPPER
1 TSP. MINCED OREGANO
1 C. RICE *(Uncooked)*
1 C. RED BEANS *(Uncooked)*
1/4 C. PINE NUTS
1/2 C. CHOPPED MANGO
* SECRET SAUCE BELOW—READ THE WHOLE THING FOR THE INGREDIENTS

Soak your beans, then cover them in water and cook until done (about 2 hours), adding more water if needed to keep them covered. Meanwhile, make your rice. When you have both, begin sautéing 1/2 C. onion, a minced chili, and 2 minced garlic cloves in 2 tsp. oil. Cook for two minutes, add beans and rice, and toss. Season to taste with cumin, saffron, chili powder, and coriander. Toss in toasted pine nuts and chopped mango, and remove from heat. Garnish when serving with fresh chopped onion and minced cilantro. For sauce, blend tomatillos, corn meal, green chilies, one onion, whole corianders, cumin seeds, oregano, lime juice and broth. Cook over medium heat for 15 minutes. Season to taste and set aside. Sauté spinach with garlic and half of the onions. Add a little cumin, chili powder and salt. Cook for three or four minutes, drain, and mix with more spice to taste, bell pepper, cilantro, crumbled tofu, and salt and pepper to taste. Add a little lime juice. Wet the tortillas in some water with lime. Roll filling in these, cover with sauce and bake at 400 for half an hour. Serve with those delicious beans and rice!

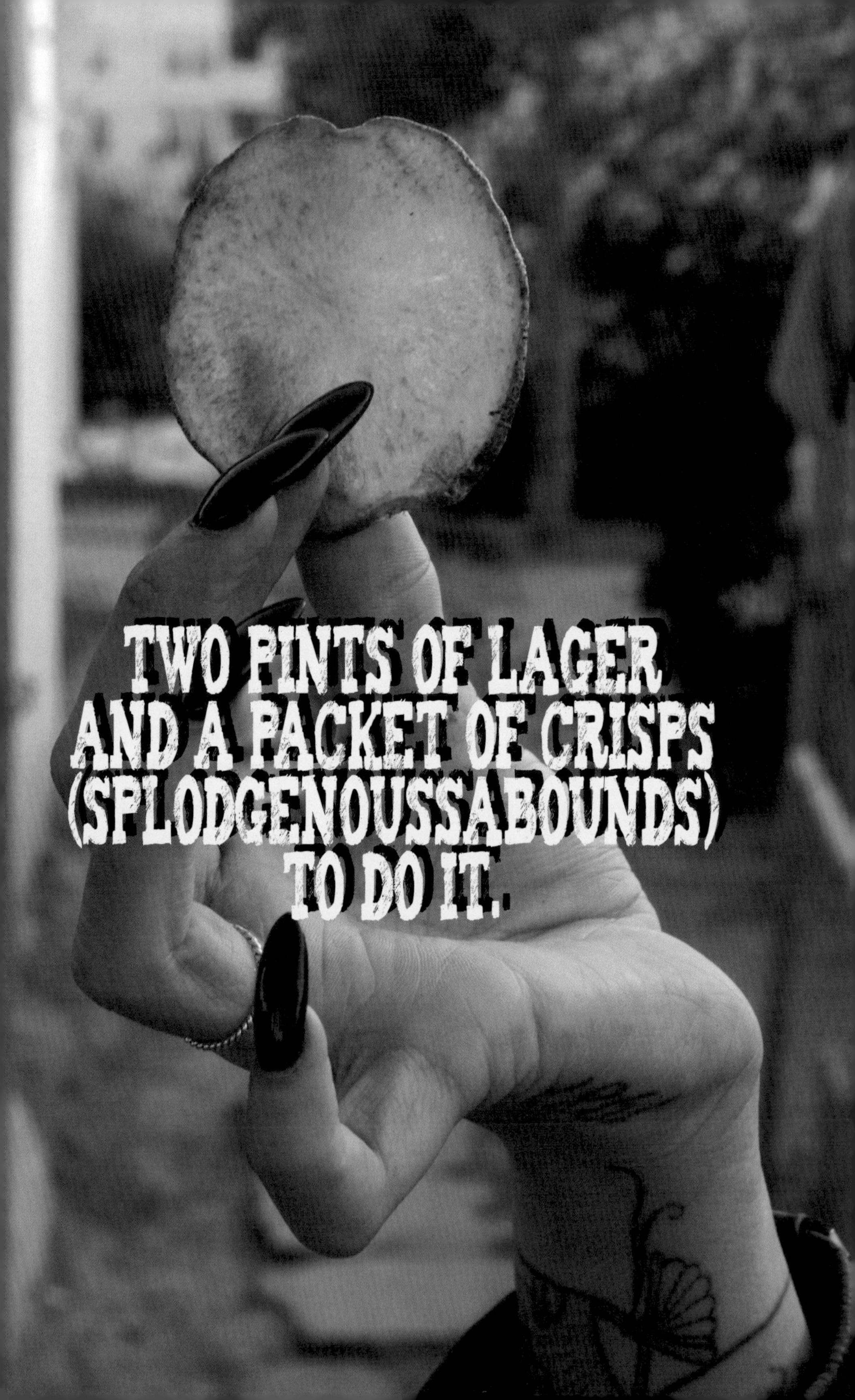

TWO PINTS OF LAGER
AND A PACKET OF CRISPS
(SPLODGENOUSSABOUNDS)
TO DO IT.

This is a cheeky number. Look up a lager recipe and spend the months it takes to make a bugger of it.
Meanwhile, chips are so easy to make and there are a couple of ways:

SEVERAL POTATOES
SEA SALT
OIL FOR FRYING

Slice the potatoes thinly and salt lightly. Fry in hot oil for several minutes, until crispy. Drain and salt. You can also fry them a bit, take them out and drain them, flatten them slightly with a spatula and then fry them again. A very crispy method. And there is also baking, coat them in oil and place on a baking sheet. Bake at 425 for 10-15 minutes, turning once until crispy.

BEEF BALONEY (FEAR, DUH!)

A bit insulting to make this vegan but hey, we punks love to insult people. This song is a pretty classic piece of work and a good candidate to be the song to play for someone who asks *"what does punk rock mean?"*

1/2 C. PIMIENTOS
1 LB. TOFU
1/2 C. TAPIOCA FLOUR
1/2 TSP. CRUSHED PEPPERCORNS
RED SALT AND TAMARI TO TASTE
2 TSP. MUSTARD
1 MINCED GARLIC CLOVE
1/4 C. CHOPPED GREEN OLIVES
1/4 C. CHOPPED ONION
1 TSP. OIL
BROTH TO COVER

Blend this together (except broth), wrap in cheesecloth and simmer in some broth for an hour or two. Drain and cool, take the cloth off and slice. Add annatto to make it more red.

DONUTS ("MMM...DONUTS" BY THE LUNACHICKS AND DOGGY STYLE'S "DONUT SHOP ROCK," AMONG OTHERS!)

2 CUPS FLOUR
1/2 CUP SUGAR
1 TSP. SALT
1 TSP. BAKING POWDER
1 PKG. DRY ACTIVE YEAST
3 TSP. MELTED COCONUT OIL
2/3 CUP WARM COCONUT MILK OR WARM WATER
1 TSP. VANILLA
1 TSP. CORN OR TAPIOCA STARCH
OIL FOR FRYING
MAKE A GLAZE BY MELTING:
4 OZ. BAKER'S CHOCOLATE
2 TSP. COCONUT MILK,
1 TSP. COCONUT OIL AND
1/4 C. BROWN SUGAR.
And have on hand some **TOASTED CHOPPED PECANS** *to sprinkle as well.*
* Optional: **DELICIOUS SHREDDED COCONUT FOR THESE TOO!!**

Activate yeast in warm coconut milk with 1 tsp. of the sugar. Mix dry ingredients together then add the wet. Form into a ball of dough and allow to rise for 30 minutes. Roll out on a floured board into a 3/8" to 1/2" thick square. Cut into 10 strips *(yes, 10 donuts?!)*. Like gnocchi, roll into ropes in the flour, keeping a decent thickness. Make into rings. Fry in hot oil until browned and delicious. Drizzle with glaze and sprinkle with nuts. This is a good job for a deep fryer. But, if you don't have one, about an inch of oil will suffice and you can just turn them when the bottoms brown. Over med/med-high heat in that case. If you want to bake donuts, donut pans are a great idea.

ROAD TRIP! 2

Thy punk rite of passage for lifers is the road trip or tour. Gas 'n dash, spangin', selling trinkets or records or performance for a pittance.

Sleeping in the van, or getting a single at a motel and cramming eight people in there. Going to stupid places we pretend not to care about like Graceland or Niagara Falls. All the while, barely able to afford to eat, and asking *"are these french fries vegan?"* I tell you what, you can make your own tasty snacks on tour *and* entertain yourself while doing it, by using the tools available to you on the road.

You'll thrill yourselves, your friends and fans while doing it, and you can even get more wild-eyed stares from the bumpkins along the way with some of these methods. And isn't that the ultimate goal? To get stared at a lot? Otherwise, you're just not doing a very good job of being punk. We're here to help!

So here's a chapter on utility cooking in the car, gas station, motel, or any mobile situation for all you touring bands and sexy groupies.

Road Trip!
by Jesse Luscious

Tour food as a genre is tough, and I give all props to the imaginative recipes that follow. For me, a non-cooking kind of person, tour food usually falls into two categories: Food provided by the promoter or gas station/diner delights.

Food provided by the promoter—whether an honest-to-goodness venue or a d.i.y. kid is putting on a cool show in a Vet's Hall or a basement—is 99% guaranteed to be either cheese pizza or spaghetti with red sauce. Being a vegetarian who hates vegetables, I love either option. My vegan bandmates are always ass-out though, unless the spaghetti comes unadorned with parmesan cheese. Two places stand out—the squats in Torino (El Paso) & Pisa. Long tables full of bands and volunteers, incredible amounts of fresh pasta, garlic bread, and all the fixings needed for a truly delicious, community-created and community-enjoyed meal. Both were the template against which I measure all such meals!

Gas stations are good for nothing but coffee. Lots and lots of coffee. Coffee snobs need to get over themselves if they're gonna go on tour. No one wants to hear about slow-drip organic free-range anarcho-socialist coffee beans at the truck stop. You want caffeine? There it is. Drink it and shut up.

Diners provide safe haven for the vegetarian (though not the vegan) with the "Grilled Cheese, Side of Fries." It's so tough to screw up a grilled cheese sandwich, I've only found one place in decades of travel that failed at this staple. Meat-eaters, good luck with the meatloaf or the grilled chicken strips—it may or may not be edible, but the grilled cheese will be excellent. Boring? Perhaps. But dangerous? Nope.

Diner salads are another danger zone—either feast or famine.

Personally, I rely on multi-vitamins to fulfill my nutritional needs on tour—between free alcohol & long food-scarce drives, my body takes a beating and I lose body fat no matter what.

The other staple I've seen work is buying sturdy food for long drives. Peanut butter works. Bread & jelly, not so much. Vegetables & fruit gather gnats when they inevitably fall on the floor and are forgotten, only to be rediscovered by whichever poor schmuck in the band is designated to clean out the van after the tour.

The key is keeping healthy and not descending into a haze of being high/drunk 24/7. I say that as a social drinker who likes to party with people at each show. Still, being aware of where you are and who you're with means that your band can find you the next morning in time to get to the next gig.

Popping pills is a bad idea on tour because it's so easy to become another sad statistic when you lose track of the day, the show, the city. Not to mention when you get pulled over, the cops will not think your bottle of pills is medically necessary, even if they are. (I always bring commercial bottles of marked multi-vitamins & aspirin)

Every so often I'd get super-hyped about going to a supermarket & stocking up—it's cheaper & healthier!—but it's never worked for me. I've been in bands with people who love to cook, and even then, the only time a supermarket run worked was when we'd be in a town for a day and we'd go out and buy food to make our hosts a big meal as a thank-you for putting up with us.

So here's to the cooks on tour. If you are one, or are in a band with one—count your lucky stars and dig in!

These songs would make a decent road mix. This will give you some insight into the way I drive. I love all of these songs, so I'll leave them without much comment.

1 - THEE HEADCOATS "HAVE LOVE WILL TRAVEL"
2 - ROLLING STONES "DOWN THE ROAD APIECE" (Inside joke.)
3 - RED AUNTS "DETROIT VALENTINE"
4 - DEAD MOON "WALKING ON MY GRAVE"
5 - BRAINBOMBS "JACK THE RIPPER LOVER"
6 - LAUGHING HYENAS "HERE WE GO AGAIN"
7 - TAD "CYANIDE BATH"
8 - SWALLOW "ZOO"
9 - KRAUT "NEW LAW"
10 - BAD BRAINS "SAILIN' ON"
11 - THE DAMNED "IGNITE"
12 - NAKED RAYGUN "RAT PATROL"
13 - DIE KREUZEN "MAN IN THE TREES"
14 - POISON IDEA "PURE HATE"
15 - D.I. "PERVERT NURSE"
16 - GERMS "LEXICON DEVIL"
17 - THE ZEROS "DON'T PUSH ME AROUND"
18 - CHRISTIAN DEATH "SPIRITUAL CRAMP"
19 - THE GUN CLUB "PREACHING THE BLUES"
20 - STOOGES "DOWN ON THE STREET"

DASHBOARD JERKY

SOME STRIPS OF CARROTS, PLANTAINS,
BEETS, TOFU, OR TEMPEH.
-MARINADE-
1/4 C. TOMATO PREPARATION (SUNDRIED
TOMATO PURÉE, TOMATO PASTE, TOMATO
SAUCE, OR MASHED TOMATO)
2 OR 3 TSP. TAMARI
HICKORY SALT AND/OR SMOKED PAPRIKA,
CHILI POWDER AND BLACK PEPPER AS
NEEDED
1 PRESSED GARLIC CLOVE
SUGAR OR OTHER SWEETENER *(if needed)*
Also, have some extra of the spices and sugar, and **HICKORY
SALT** *reserved and make a tasty mix of this for extra coating later, if
desired.*

Mix up the **MARINADE**. Dredge the vegetable/tofu strips through this and then place on foil on the dash facing direct sunlight. A single layer with a little space between the items is desirable. You also don't want them to be too wet. As you drive into the sun, turn them once every hour or so. They will dehydrate a fair amount during this time. When you're ready, dredge them in the spice mix and devour. The drying time is quite long, around 4- 6 hours depending on how hot it is up there and the texture you're looking for. Obviously, it won't be all dried out like some processed thing, but rather strangely cooked! Hah!

Without the marinade on it, it will dry more expeditiously but why not make your long-ass drive more entertaining. Direct sunlight on a dashboard easily reaches 120 or more in the summer time. This is great for those of you without air conditioning. Passenger side eastbound is ideal, where the sun will be on it for that amount of time.

Hello Texas! If you want to be more complicated, soak the strips in marinade awhile before placing on the dashboard foil. This increases the drying time however.

DASHBOARD KALE CHIPS

1 HEAD KALE, BROKEN INTO PIECES
SALT
FOIL

This is too easy: Place kale on foil on the dashboard and allow to sit in the sun for several hours, turning occasionally, until fairly crispy. Salt to taste. Same diff as the concept above, basically.

SNACK BAR SALAD

Here's an idea, try to make something vaguely healthy out of what you can find in a gas station. Something like a waldorf can be achieved. Doing this sort of thing used to be the failed dream of many touring folks but now you can. Thanks modern society!

2 BANANAS, SLICED
2 DICED APPLES
1 C. SMOKED ALMONDS
1 C. CHOPPED BABY CARROTS
1/2 C. RAISINS OR CRANBERRIES
A FEW TSP. POMEGRANATE JUICE OR OTHER REFRESHING JUICY BEVERAGE *(don't scoff, pomegranate crap is everywhere)*
how about some of those **SPICY CHILI LIMA BEANS***!?*
SALT AND PEPPER TO TASTE
* MORE OPTIONS—PEANUTS, PIECES OF CHOCOLATE, COCONUT, AND PINEAPPLE
(you can pick it out of the trail mix)

Ooh what an interesting mix, it's almost gourmet. Toss together and serve in an ashtray. If they have acoutrements for burgers and "nachos," then oh look out you can start adding jalapenos, onions, tomatoes, maybe even lettuce! Salsa to add to your dressing, olives, all kinds of garbage...

ENGINE BLOCK CASSEROLE

Now this of course if done wrong could be a disaster. Watch a couple of videos how to before attempting or ask a pro. Also, yes the type of car makes a difference, so check around for your brand to be repped. For example, in many cars the exhaust manifold is a good hot spot for cooking. Somewhere out there someone must have a food car(t) where the vehicle cooks all the food. The health defartment would probably be bummed. Oh well! Lots of bands bake potatoes and sweet potatoes on the engine. Works great! Classic stuff!

1 THINLY SLICED SWEET POTATO
1 HEAD KALE
2 SLICED PORTOBELLO MUSHROOMS
1/2 LB. THINLY SLICED SMOKED TOFU
SALT AND PEPPER
1/4 C. LEMON JUICE
CHILI POWDER
SUNDRIED TOMATOES
1/2 C. PECANS
2 PEELED GARLIC CLOVES
1/2 C. SLICED RED ONION
2 TSP. OLIVE OIL
1/2 C. BASIL LEAVES

Blend pecans, olive oil, basil, garlic, sundried tomatoes, and lemon juice with salt to taste. Layer with the other ingredients in a small metal tray or thick aluminum foil, alternating between veggies and pesto, sprinkling with salt, pepper and chili powder here and there. Wrap tightly in foil, being careful that it's good and tight and any seams will be on top. Then wrap it again. To cook this you will want to find a hot, flat place in the engine. You will probably want to secure it with some wire and clamps if you can. Should take an hour or so driving around. I don't mean tooting around town either. I mean a real drive. Remember, you don't want it falling, blocking anything important, or leaking AT ALL, so take all due precautions. And if you fuck it up, well don't blame me because *no one should ever cook on their engine!* Haha! How's that for a disclaimer? Thanks, America!

ZIPPO S'MORES

This is the idiot savant's mainly idiotic method. Basically, you're gonna burn yourself. But if you're like me and love to burn your fingers all the time, this is *perfect* for you. Except, don't EVER try this EVER! Kids, you can't read so I don't have to worry about you, but when you see the video, never ever imitate something that someone else does successfully that looks fun. Ever! Because insurance and morals and death and stuff. I don't like marshmallows, so I'm gonna have you make fluff instead.

-GRAHAM CRACKER-
1 3/4 C. GRAHAM FLOUR
1/2 C. ALL-PURPOSE FLOUR
1/3 C. DARK BROWN SUGAR
3/4 TEASPOON BAKING POWDER
1/2 TEASPOON BAKING SODA
1/2 TEASPOON SALT *(more to taste)*
1/4 TEASPOON GROUND CINNAMON
6 TSP. UNSALTED "BUTTER," CUT INTO 1/4-INCH CUBES AND CHILLED
2 TSP. MOLASSES
2 TSP. SOY OR OTHER "MILK"
1/2 TEASPOON VANILLA EXTRACT
1/2 TSP. POWDERED GINGER
"YOU SHOULD USE 'FUCK' IN YOUR BOOK AS MUCH AS POSSIBLE" —FOREHEAD (OGRE SMASH DEATH BOOM)

-FLUFF-
1/4 C. CORN SYRUP
1/4 C. POWDERED SUGAR
1 TSP. TAPIOCA OR CORNSTARCH
1 TSP. SOY LECITHIN
PINCH OF SALT
1 TSP. COCONUT OIL
1/2 TSP. VANILLA

YOU WILL ALSO NEED:
THIN SQUARES OF DARK CHOCOLATE

Mix the dry ingredients of the graham cracker, then crumb in the margarine. Add the wet and form into a ball. Chill for a little bit then roll out to 1/4" thickness *(or a bit less, if you can)*. Place on baking parchment lined baking sheets and score into cracker size desired. Poke some nifty pattern in with a fork.

Bake at 350 for 25 minutes. Cool pans on wire racks and break/cut into crackers when completely cooled.

Heat corn syrup to bubbling. Frantically whisk the salt, oil, and cornstarch into the syrup. Remove from heat and whisk everything else in. You need to go at it for several minutes. Allow to cool down before using. Some coconut cream or silken tofu or other creamy stuff can also be added, or more tapioca to achieve different textures, but basically sugar, vanilla, and a tad of salt will make it taste marshmallow-y.

A spoon of marshmallow goop, square of chocolate, and two crackers make one s'more.

Hold together carefully and run your lighter around the edge, get up in there to start up some meltiness. Be careful not to burn the crap out of yourself. Obviously a wand works better. Takes some work. Keep your sleeves short and do it over a sink or concrete so you don't burn down the place.

SOAKED THAI NOODLES

Anything that can be soaked rather than cooked is pretty much awesome. Especially if you are living out of a van, motel room, couch, or other crappy situation. You could eat something like this every day, changing around the ingredients. And yes, they can also be totally cold soaked, it just takes a little longer.

1 PKG. RICE NOODLES
1 OR 2 BELL PEPPERS, SLICED THINLY
1 LB. CHOPPED SEASONED TOFU OR OTHER
1/2 C. ROASTED PEANUTS OR CASHEWS
1 C. SLICED NAPA OR RED CABBAGE
3 OR 4 MINCED SCALLIONS
1 TSP. GRATED GINGER
2 GRATED CARROTS
1/2 C. GRATED JICAMA OR DAIKON
(more if you like)
1 OR 2 MINCED FRESH CHILIES
SEVERAL TSP. HOISIN OR GARLIC SAUCE *(or another interesting sauce)*
LIME JUICE TO TASTE
HANDFUL OF CHOPPED THAI BASIL
HANDFUL OF CHOPPED MINT
* OTHER ADDITIONS: LEMONGRASS, GALANGAL, GREEN PAPAYA, RIBBONS OF ROMAINE

Soak rice noodles in hot water from the tap until soft, this could take anywhere from 10 to half an hour. Use the ice bucket, coffee pot, or *(gasp!)* sink. Drain when ready, toss with the other ingredients, and season to taste.

PS—Whenever using the sink to soak, never ever do that! And don't tell the health department.

COFFEE POT CURRY

Here we select veggies that are fine warm rather than boiled. I have to do this, or coffee pot blanching, quite a bit. Hope they never take the ol' coffee maker out of motels because they are pretty darn useful. You can adjust amounts of liquid and try different things and see what happens.

1 C. SLICED MUSHROOMS
1 HEAD CHOPPED GREENS
1/2 C. CHOPPED ONION
2 MINCED GARLIC CLOVES
2 DICED CARROTS
1 CHOPPED BELL PEPPER
(RED OR GREEN OR A MIX)
1 C. COCONUT MILK
2 TSP. CURRY POWDER
1/2 LB. CHOPPED TOFU OR
OTHER IF YOU LIKE
SALT AND PEPPER TO TASTE
A HANDFUL OF CHOPPED CILANTRO OR BASIL
1 C. BROTH OR WATER

Place everything but the coconut milk and
water/brothn the coffee pot.
Pour broth/water into the back/tank and turn it on,
making sure to put the pot on the burner. After
the broth has sprayed into the pot,
give it a stir and let sit for several minutes.
Add coconut milk, season and stir occasionally,
allowing it to warm through on the burner.
20 minutes should suffice.

3

NECESSITY IS
THE MOTHER
OF SOMETHING
OF SOMETHING
SOMETHING

We are an innovative people.

If something is absent, there are two ways of dealing with it...and things are absent a lot of the time, like when you're on the road!

1) To stand around for hours like a stoner waiting for "the guy with the PA that's a friend of my friend" to show up or...

2) To get shit started like a real punk rocker and make it happen! With or without, let's do this!

No mic? Use a bullhorn!
No bass? Play a guitar or a tuba!
No audience? Play anyway!
No hair gel? Use pitch or tar!
                    (just kidding)

And it works for cooking as well...
No plate? Use a frisbee!
No baking pan? Do it on the stovetop! Missing something? Replace it!
No oven? Microwave! Haha

Punks get innovative when missing ingredients, gear, or an oven... now you can too!

Necessity is the Mother of Something Something

by Ilsa Hess

I grew up thinking that I didn't have a voice in the world, and these punks helped me realize that I could make a difference. I realized I didn't have to buy the stuff corporations like Macy's and McDonalds were telling me I needed in order to fit in. I realized it was more fun to shop at thrift stores, eat veg, and be aware of what corporations did to our country.

But it wasn't until college that I started getting into the political and DIY aspects of the scene. A local punk, Jason Kirkpatrick, and his friends were part of Food Not Bombs in Arcata, CA, and opened me up to all the reasons why people need to be vegan. Being vegan is giving the finger to Big Agriculture and all the food corporations force feeding us propaganda about how meat and dairy are good for you. Such bullshit! Jason took a stand and became the mayor of Arcata in 1994. I was blown away and totally inspired. With some DIY energy, you actually can make this world a better place!

Enter: solar cooking. Off-the-grid solar cooking is one of my favorite ways to continue to show my punk and DIY roots. Not to mention that making your own solar cooker is a great way to show off your many punk rock skills. Reuse a pile of junk slated for the garbage and create an almost-free cooking machine! Hell yeah! Spray paint, "PG&E: Take your gas and shove it!" on the side of the solar cooker for a lovely final touch.

If you are on the road and don't want to lug your solar cooking masterpiece around, don't fret! Reuse that piece of foil from your burrito wrap and put it on your dash. Voila! Your car is now a solar cooker/dehydrator. Yes, it's that easy.

I was camping before I was born, literally. My parents camped since the day they met and conceived me while camping. TMI? Tell me about it. Anyway, camping taught me a lot about finding creative solutions to things I wanted to do while out in the wilderness. I love things that have more than one purpose. Swiss Army Knives fascinate me. The punk/DIY ethic and my love for living off the land continues to fuel my Ms. Gyver (the feminine of MacGyver) skills.

Nothing is more punk rock than figuring out a creative way to cook a cheap-ass vegan meal on the road or improvising equipment in an inadequate kitchen. For me, it's the shaded part where all the circles of a crazy complex Venn diagram intertwine. So many ideals I have learned in my life intersect in the punk scene. Joshua and his traveling vegan chef ways have shown me that being creative is fun. There's no reason you can't be a gourmet punk on the road. Enjoy!

The super-DIY chapter requires a super DIY bunch of bands, these people all throw shows (or used to), do cool shit, or run record labels, and are all around nice people. No wait, we're supposed to be punk so they're mean. They're real, *real* mean!

1 -FRIENDS FOREVER (Look up video of them playing out of their van to start the playlist out, but really you had to be there.)

2- TEAM DRESCH "HAND GRENADE"

3- HIGH PLACES "ALL THE DAYS BLUR TOGETHER" (With David Scott Stone, so this is a multi-layered selection.)

4- DUFFY & THE BEER SLAYERS "SPACE BEAR" (They will take care of all of your North Dakota needs.)

5- HUASIPUNGO "OI POR HOY" (My bands have never played at ABC NoRio, but I did cook there once—it was really hot and people were scared to eat the food.)

6- PALATKA "THE STATE OF 6PM"

7- SMD "NEVER GONNA CHANGE" (Maybe Rito will let you play at his house.)

8- IMPETUS INTER "DON'T CARE MUCH ABOUT PLACES"

9- WITCHY POO "OLYMPIA MUST DIE" (They ought to know.)

10- MY LAI "QUESTION OF IMAGE" (Fireside Bowl!!)

11- NEEDLES "DESPERACION"

12- CAPTAIN CHAOS "AT LEAST IT'S NOT AN ALLIGATOR" (This guy!)

13- MOLDY PEACHES "GREYHOUND BUS" (If you don't think Kimya is a punk I guess you've never been with her in the pit or been to the shitty punk houses she had to live in then)

14- JESUS FUCKING CHRIST "SADISTIC MADNESS" (Larryyyyyyyy!!!)

15- TRACY & THE PLASTICS "THE MYTH OF THE FRONT"

16- BRATMOBILE "THE REAL JANELLE" (Two or three birds with one stone on this one! I should put one of Janelle's bands on here—I think I still have that Lumps tape somewhere)

17- THE CRIMINALS "I WANNA STAB YOU WITH SOMETHING RUSTY"

18- BEAT HAPPENING "MIDNIGHT A GOGO"

19- PARTY OF HELICOPTERS "THE TOUCHER" (Cuddly.)

20- THE POTATOMEN "ALL MY YESTERDAYS"

21- THE EVAPORATORS "UNITED EMPIRE LOYALISTS" (Nardwuar is just a fun all-around guy.)

CREDIT CARD CHOPPING

I happened on this method of cutting things while on a boat to Greece which is perhaps not the most punk rock setting ever. Gambling, chainsmoking EU truckers probably don't give a shit what is punk or not though, and that is largely who populated this ship. Nonetheless, the concept is pretty great. Don't tell the dipshits at TSA and all the fearful turds out there, or they'll ban cards next! Even paper cuts can be hella deep!

Do you dare me to cut things with paper too? I can. I swear. Use card stock, you can totally chop garlic with it. Great for troubleshooting. Sometimes there just ain't a knife around!

-CREDIT CARD SANDWICH-
CRUSTY ITALIAN BREAD
1 AVOCADO
1 TOMATO
RED ONION
ARUGULA
A FEW TBSP. MUSTARD
CHILI SAUCE

-PESTO-
1/2 C. NUTS
JUICE OF 1 LEMON
HANDFUL OF CHOICE OF HERBS
SALT TO TASTE
3 OR 4 PEELED GARLIC CLOVES
2-3 TBSP. OLIVE OIL

Chop and slice everything using a credit card or similar item. Mix the pesto ingredients together once chopped/minced. Toast the bread if you like then layer with all of these fabulous ingredients.

CURRY BANANA SANDWICHES

This will be familiar to people that own my other books, but self-referencing and plagiarism are punk as fuck!

BANANAS
1 TBSP. LIME JUICE
1/4 C. MINCED RED OR GREEN BELL PEPPER
HALF OF A MINCED CHILI PEPPER
1/2 TO 1 TSP. CURRY POWDER, DEPENDING ON TASTE
A FEW TBSP. CILANTRO OR PARSLEY
3 MINCED SCALLIONS
SALT AND PEPPER TO TASTE
SLICED BREAD

Make sure you do all of your mincing and chopping with the credit card. Mix all but the bread gently with your paws. Or a spoon. Season/adjust to taste, and use for sandwich.

USING INTERESTING TOOLS IN THE KITCHEN

Sometimes you just don't have the fancy stuff to cut things properly, but you do have other tools.

Woodworking tools *(as pictured previously)*, pens/pen casings *(just take the works out)*, other interesting shavers, boring tools, screwdrivers, and fingernail cutters are among the various tools that can be used to shave, ribbon, and do other amusing cuts on veggies. Just wash it thoroughly and let imagination be your limit. Even a tape dispenser could be used for creative peeling and scoring—why not!? How about the eye of a large needle? Yep! Just be careful of course.

Really I can't emphasize enough that what you have lying around could most likely be easily used or modified for culinary purposes. Trust me.

How many times has someone told me they don't have a basting brush but then they had paintbrushes that they'd never used? Or that were clean—really!? What are you, the kitchen quarantine man? Come on, a brush is a brush as long as it's not some toxic crap!! Also, you can of course use your fingers, a paper towel, or a piece of plastic wrap or paper bag to baste or brush as well.

You can use a dropper as a baster. You can use a can with the lids cut off as a ring mold.

What can't you do?! Take a look in the drawers around the house. Seriously, get punk!

BEER TEMPURA

THINLY SLICED SWEET POTATO
CAULIFLOWER FLORETS
BROCCOLI FLORETS
WHEELS OF SLICED ONION
OKRA

-BATTER-
SALT AND PEPPER TO TASTE
1 1/2 C. ANY FLOUR
SEVERAL TSP. CORN STARCH, TAPIOCA, OR
OTHER STARCH *(optional)*
1 C. BEER *(more as needed)*
I LIKE CURRY POWDER IN THERE
OIL FOR FRYING

Mix **BATTER** ingredients together, you want it to have a pancake batter-like consistency.

Season the vegetables a bit (chili, salt, black pepper, favorite spice mix—that sort of thing) and toss in a bowl with the other goop until well coated.

Fry in hot oil *(you don't really need a lot)*, turning once, until browned on both sides. You can also bake them of course. I'd go for 425 on a greased baking sheet for 15 minutes, turn and cook for another 10-15 minutes.

MARINADE WILTING AND CURING

You can mimic cooking with a marinade, a trick of both preserving and raw cuisine. Get creative! *(You can slip these past people that normally don't love raw mushrooms.)*

MUSHROOMS:

Rinse the mushrooms lightly and drain. Place them in a plastic bag with some smoked or flavored salt and shake. Set in the fridge for a bit, then shake again. You don't need tons of salt to do this. After an hour or more they can seem strangely cooked. What will overnight do? I use this method for raw stuffed mushrooms.

KALE PARTICULARLY (OR OTHER GREENS):

Massaging and dressing kale are popular methods of preparation. Just take the ribs out and rub the pieces together. Salt and a little olive oil can be used as well in small quantities to assist. Do this for a few minutes. Wait, and then repeat. It's easier to use in a number of raw ways after doing this. Takes the edge off, that's for sure!

ONIONS:

Marinate raw sliced onions in just a little balsamic or cider vinegar and a few pinches of salt. The longer they sit in there, the softer and less raw they will be. Raw onion haters can be placated by this method at least briefly haha! Let your imagination run wild!!

SAUCEPAN CORNBREAD

Sometimes it seriously just sucks to turn on the oven, or maybe
the oven's not working but your stovetop is. Cornbread is an
easy thing to make in a skillet, in fact this is often a preferred method.

1 1/2 C. CORNMEAL
1/2 C. FLOUR (OR SORGHUM FLOUR)
2 TSP. AGAVE OR MAPLE SYRUP
1/2 C. CORN
2 TSP. BAKING POWDER

1/2 TO 1 TSP. SALT *(depending on your taste)*
3 TSP. OIL
1/2 TSP. CHILI POWDER
1 TSP. LEMON JUICE
1 1/4 C. ALMOND MILK OR SOY MILK OR SUCH

Mix the ingredients together and pour into a greased skillet over medium
heat. It's a good idea to have a little wire separator between the burner and
the pan to prevent burning. Cover and cook for 20 minutes or so. You can
lower the heat if you need to. Keep an eye on it. You can even flip it, as some
people do.

MICROWAVE BLANCHING

In a pinch, a microwave is useful for cooking rice and quinoa. It is also useful to blanch, cook down, or par cook a number of items. Such as:

GREENS:

Simply wash the leaves and lay them on a plate while still a bit damp. You can cover with a microwave-proof cloth or something, but it's not necessary. Nuke for 2 minutes, allow to cool briefly then reorder them and do it for 1 minute longer. They will be useable for rolling this way, without being raw *(for collard rolls or other items)*. The less you microwave them, the more lightly they will be cooked. This works for most vegetables, if you slice and cook them, covered with only a little water it doesn't take very long for them to steam or blanch in there. Keep an eye for variability from appliance to appliance.

POTATOES AND SWEET POTATOES:

Can also be par-cooked for easy frying (wash, poke holes, and cook for 2-3 minutes per side for several potatoes). Or "baked" which can fool anyone. This varies wildly timewise from microwave to microwave. You can wash and poke holes with a fork in several potatoes and sweet potatoes, and then microwave them for 4-6 minutes per side usually. Sweet potatoes (if they are not huge) are more like 3-4 per side. That means you turn them once, folks!
Again, depending on the number of them you're trying to do and the power of the microwave, it can take more or less time. Poke with a fork or knife occasionally to see if they are tender.

STOVETOP SMOKING

Smoking on the stovetop is pretty dang easy. You just have to
pay attention. It doesn't smoke to the extent that a regular
smoker does but it gets the job done. If you have a super
sensitive fire alarm, you probably shouldn't do it. DO NOT leave
it unattended. At all. You can also do this outside over coals
using a similar theory as long as you can keep the smoke largely contained.

**LARGE POT WITH LID
METAL STEAMER
ALUMINUM FOIL
2-3 TSP. OR SO WOOD SHAVINGS—ALDER,
MAPLE, OR APPLE OR SOMETHING.** *You don't need
"official wood chips," but if you are making your own, make sure
there is no debris (such as nails) or chemicals involved. Cook for 5
min. on higher heat, 10-15 on lower.*

**YOU CAN COOK:
A HALF LB. OF MUSHROOMS
A LB. OR TWO OF TOFU OR TEMPEH
SLICED EGGPLANT**

Place a piece of foil in the bottom of your pot. Lay the wood chips on top of this,
followed by another layer of foil. Next goes your metal steamer. In the steamer
place what you want to smoke, in a single layer (slightly overlapping is okay).
Place the lid on top and cover/seal the edge thoroughly with foil, you definitely
do not want smoke getting out of the pot. Cook on high heat for around 5
minutes to get it started, then drop to medium low for 20-30 minutes. Let
the pot sit for 10-15 minutes with the smoke in there. When you finally remove
the lid, you might want to do it out back. And keep your face out of there.
Potholders are your friend. You can use marinated items beforehand of course,
you just don't want that dripping all over the place in the smoker, so make sure
there's not ass-tons of liquid still on your food when you throw it in there.

STOVETOP PIZZA

"IT ISN'T GOOD FOOD IF I DON'T BURP AND FART AFTERWARDS"
- FOREHEAD (OGRE SMASH DEATH BOOM)

-DOUGH-

2/3 C. WARM WATER (more or less as needed)
2 ENVELOPES RAPID RISE YEAST
1 TSP. SALT (more or less to your taste)
2 TSP. OLIVE OIL
1 TSP. GARLIC POWDER OR GRANULATED GARLIC
1/4 C. CORNMEAL
2 C. OF FLOUR (possibly more)
UNBLEACHED WHITE is best, or you can make a blend (just make sure it isn't crumbly—if you're doing wheat free, it can be the consistency of thick pancake batter, just spread it in the pan with a rubber spatula and flip when the bottom is cooked/browned, then continue following the normal instructions)

-SAUCE-

1/2 C. TOMATO PASTE
A FEW TSP. CHILI SAUCE
A LITTLE OIL
MINCED GARLIC AND HERBS, as you like
SALT AND PEPPER TO TASTE
A LITTLE OLIVE JUICE AND BALSAMIC VINEGAR
WATER to bring it to the consistency of a thick marinara
* optional—some **SOY CHORIZO** mixed in there. It's quite good.
* optional—**1 OR 2 TSP. ZAHTER** So good!

-SUGGESTED TOPPINGS-

If you prefer them cooked, cook vegetables before adding to the pizza.
I suggest:
SAUTÉED MUSHROOMS
CARAMELIZED RED ONIONS
CHOPPED OLIVES
WILTED SPINACH WITH GARLIC
SEARED BROCCOLINI WITH SEASONED SALT
RED PEPPER FLAKES
THIN CRISPY FRIED POTATOES SEASONED WITH HICKORY, CHILI POWDER, AND GARLIC SALT
And that makes a good pizza in any combination!

* try a handful of **ARUGULA** added on there, wilt by covering or have fresh on the warm pizza!

-CONDIMENTS TO DRIZZLE AND DOT-

- BARBEQUE SAUCE WITH MARINARA
- VEGAN CREAM CHEESE, MARINARA, MUSTARD, AND A LITTLE VODKA MIXED TOGETHER

- **PURÉED OLIVES WITH CAPERS, GARLIC, HERBS, AND OLIVE OIL**
- **CHILI SAUCE WITH VEGAN SOUR CREAM, GARLIC, AND LEMON JUICE**
- **TAMARIND SAUCE, CHILI SAUCE, AND CURRY SAUCE MIXED TOGETHER**
- **YOUR FAVORITE NUTRITIONAL YEAST, MISO, PEPPER CASHEW, OR OTHER UNCHEESE SAUCEMIXED WITH YOUR SECOND FAVORITE UNCHEESE SAUCE**
- **BECHAMEL WITH HERBS, GARLIC, ONION, A LITTLE MUSTARD,** *(with a relish to be a bit more like remoulade)*
- **PECAN-SAGE PESTO SAUCE OR HAZELNUT-BASIL-THYME PESTO SAUCE**
- **MOLE OR SOME BEAUTIFUL CHUTNEY**

Get into preparing and mixing various condiments together. Experiment! It's fun!

For the **CRUST**, dissolve yeast in warm water and stir, and let sit for 10-15 minutes to activate. Mix in the rest, adding more flour if needed, to make a pliable pizza dough *(if doing GF, use pancake batter method above)*. Knead for a few minutes, then place in a bowl in a warm place, cover with a cloth loosely and let rise for 45 minutes or more. Mix the **SAUCE** ingredients together, adjusting the liquidity as you see fit. Roll out a handful sized ball of pizza dough *(or slightly bigger)* on a floured board with some cornmeal, into about an 11" or 12" circle or square. Sprinkle with a little garlic powder on both sides as well. Coat a 12" skillet with oil *(well coated, but don't deep fry the poor thing. It can also be done without oil.)* and heat to medium or medium high. Place the crust on there and cook until the bottom is browned/done to your liking. Now flip the bugger over and the bottom becomes the top. Coat with a healthy layer of pizza sauce, array toppings, drizzle with your sauces, and cook until done on the bottom. If the toppings need re-heating, place a bell or upside down pan over the cooking pan for most of the remaining cooking time, and they will heat in a satisfactory manner. A little black on the bottom isn't so bad *(but please, don't overdo it)*, if you're into coal-fired pizzas it will give a familiar taste that you will enjoy. Just be a little careful when you take it out of the pan, it might appear slightly floppy at first but should still be sliceable.

WHAT CAN YOU MAKE FROM A BAG OF FLOUR AND LITTLE ELSE?

Flour is very versatile. You only need a few other things to make something out of it. Sometimes it's all ya got. I once fed two people for 2 weeks on 25 bucks worth of stuff. The bag of flour was an indespensible part of the festivities. I know it gets a bad rap these days but don't let that get to ya!

-FRYBREAD-
1 C. FLOUR
1/4 TO 1/2 TSP. SALT *(taste dependent)*
1 TSP. BAKING POWDER *(baking soda can be used or use 1/4 C. soda or beer for some of the water)*
1/3 TO 1/2 C. WATER
A LITTLE GARLIC POWDER *won't kill it*
you can add **A BIT OF SUGAR** *if you like*
OIL FOR FRYING *(you really don't need a lot)*

Mix the dry ingredients together then add the wet to make a workable dough. Break pieces off and flatten them on a lightly floured board with your hands. They should be about 1/4" thick. Fry in hot/med high oil in a skillet, turning once, until browned on both sides. For gluten free, a similar method works—you will prob need xanthan gum or cornstarch or tapioca to make it pliable by the hands *(and maybe a little oil)*, or you can make it a bit wetter and do a drop batter *(again though, starch or gum is advisable)*.

-FLATBREAD-
1 1/2 TSP. DRY YEAST
1 C. WARM WATER
1 TSP. SUGAR
3 C. FLOUR
1 TSP. SALT *(or to taste)*
2 TSP. OIL *(not necessary)*
1 TSP. LEMON JUICE *(optional)*
you can add **GARLIC FLAKES, PARSLEY, CILANTRO, SCALLIONS,** *or other herbs, or all of them!*

Activate the yeast with warm water and sugar. Add oil, salt, and lemon juice if you're using them. Work in the flour and any herbs you want to use to make a dough ball. Knead for several minutes. Let stand covered in a warm place for an hour or two. Tear pieces out and roll them out very thin on a floured board. Cook, turning once, in a dry skillet on medium until browned on both sides. You'll have to do it one at a time obviously and may have to wipe or clean the pan out periodically to keep excess flour from burning and smoking up the place. Each side will only take about 2 minutes to cook.

-PANCAKES-

1 C. FLOUR
1 C. WATER OR YOUR FAVORITE MILK
1 TSP. SUGAR *(optional)*
2 TSP. OIL OR MELTED MARGARINE OR
COCONUT OIL
1 TSP. BAKING POWDER (OR...)
1/2 TSP. SALT *(more or less to taste)*

Optional stuff:
*FRUIT, JAM, OR SYRUP TO TOP
*SPICES *(not necessary but can jazz things up, cinnamon and nutmeg particularly)*
*ADD A TSP. VANILLA *(big improvement)*
use leftovers you can put in there, like COOKED RICE, COOKED
MAC N CHEESE, COOKED CURRIES *(yeah, re-make, re-model!)*

Mix the ingredients together and drop 1/4 to 1/2 C.'s of batter onto lightly greased pan, spread and cook, flipping once, until browned on both sides. I always do medium heat.

-DUMPLINGS-

2 C. FLOUR

2 TSP. BAKING POWDER *(or use soda water or beer for part of the liquid, or use baking soda)*

1 TSP. SALT

1 TSP. CIDER VINEGAR *(optional) Why? For that ol' buttermilk-style flavor.*

1 1/4 C. WATER, BROTH, OR SOY OR OTHER MILK

ONION POWDER *is nice but not necessary.*

Option: you can add cooked mashed potatoes to the dumpling batter in some quantity and fairly mimic gnocchi which wouldbe a funny thing for your poor ass to be serving up.

If you go out foraging maybe you could make gnocchi with wilted dandelions, herbs, and flowers. Hahaha—poor my ass!

Technically you wouldn't be bothering with baking powder or as much liquid to make gnocchi and they are supposed to be mostly potato. But whatever, do what you wish.

Mix the dry ingredients, then add the wet. Mix to make a nice dough. Form balls with your hands and drop into simmering salt and peppered water or broth, and cook for 20 minutes or until done.

If you add some vegetables to the pot as you go, you're making a stew, otherwise take them out with a slotted spoon and serve with gravy or other sauces. You can also, of course, make biscuits and gravy but I shant bore you yet again with that one!

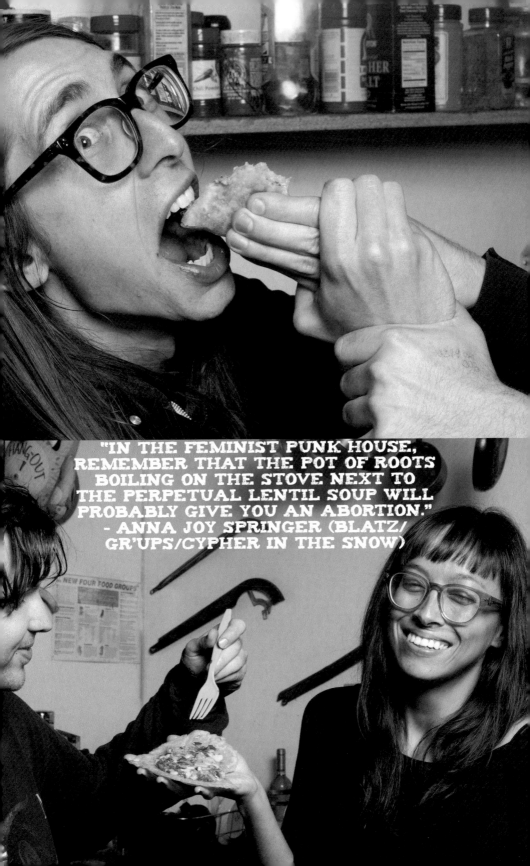

"IN THE FEMINIST PUNK HOUSE,
REMEMBER THAT THE POT OF ROOTS
BOILING ON THE STOVE NEXT TO
THE PERPETUAL LENTIL SOUP WILL
PROBABLY GIVE YOU AN ABORTION."
- ANNA JOY SPRINGER (BLATZ/
GR'UPS/CYPHER IN THE SNOW)

4 THE DAY TURNED

Originally much of what punk was about or perceived as, had to do with their clothes.

Shocking, impractical, ambitious, or just plain ridiculous.

It was pretty good stuff, eventually degenerating into various uniforms. Or alternately, with hardcore, they don't bother with outfits at all, yet somehow they have the same jeans, tennis shoes, and black shirt. And it was played off like some great reaction to punk fashion, gettin' all down to business and "real," and yet this attitude really is just terribly boring.

THE KITCHEN
DAY-GLO

Why not just play naked (I might go check that out, depending on which dudes)?

Anyway, it was a sad day when we all started to look alike. There was a time when each punk weirdo looked freakier than the next.
Let's bring it back, sexy!

What will I wear to the revolution? It's the question that should be on every punk's mind. And that goes for your plate as well. Pretty on the outside, pretty on the inside!

Punk color, fashion, and flavor come to life in your kitchen.

The Day The Kitchen Turned Day-Glo

by Monica Sklar

Punk fashion is a visual and embodied statement that can be artistic, political, regional, cultural, subtle and bombastic. The DIY element of punk is seen in the way food is approached today. After years of processed and pre-packaged, the "real" always reigns as the most important, the most healthy, and the real deal is not too hard to spot in apparel or food.

Whether it was the Ramones's t-shirts, jeans, and Converse with their timeless and effortless cool, or the Bromley Contingent's carefully and enthusiastically crafted walking art projects; both demonstrate care. The classic burger and a 4-star meal both register high in our satisfaction and sense of authenticity. Punk fashion is about attitude, argot, and inherent questioning and this is very true of food, especially now, as we must consider what we are eating, how we are consuming, and whether our plate has soul.

The style of punk, like food, has a heritage, and yet it's constantly evolving. Without its past it would not have a foundation and would not have references to draw upon which link together the culture and provide a backdrop of how things prior were started. It is often referential in its details and yet each individual adds specific character. The tartan plaid, that fashionably reimagined a British past, is akin to the slow food, whole grain that is recontextualizing our present. Fashion and food continues to be shaped by cultural needs and each region, economic up and down swing, and influential voice present new ideas to resonate loudly and hopefully shake our insides like a crowded basement show.

The tattered clothes of punk, often imperfect on purpose, are allowed to be emboldened by their shreds from experience.

The ripped fishnets and stained hoodie are perfectly thought out even if thrown on, because the pieces are all part of a wardrobe of conscious. The best food has great intentions and isn't belabored to the point of not letting it shine on its own. It is about intention with a willingness to be flexible in the result and its interpretation. Accents or garnish adds variety and personalization. Accessories are the little details that pinpoint nuances; a splash of green cilantro or a twist of a lemon peel; a one inch button with art of that too short masterwork or a decorative headband with a DIY felt flower. While punk style is known for its desire to stand out, to reach out, it's not always about being blatant. Subtlety with a grand accent can do the trick. A conventional outfit with unnatural hair color, funky colored Vans, or a skinny neon tie. In crafting a dish, a flavor bomb overwhelms, it's too over the top and trying too hard. Both strive for that perfect blend that is speaking to many people in general terms and to some very intimately.

Color is one of the most informative and, at times, thrilling aesthetic elements. It's a place in food and clothes to highlight and personalize. The expressive characteristics of color create a visceral reaction when our feelings come in an instant. Color themes and layers of meaning run true as we peruse the co-op to the mega-mall on our quest to consume and utilize items that somehow reflect our identity. We have gut reactions to the colors of our food and our clothes and mine also for understanding in their hues. The punk palette of black, red, silver, and neons impacts our decisions, and is rooted in reference and instinct. The engaging and dark hues that are also included in the punk wardrobe are frequently seen in the most appealing of food; lush green, beet red, and blood orange; rich with nutrients. Dark shades are introspective as they absorb all light and nourish us with their mysteries we just have to unravel. Attention-getting brights tempt us to experiment and heighten the senses. The allure of a red fishnet; a drizzle of raspberry coulis. All constructed in the metals of the world around us, symbols of industry from spikes and studs to pots and pans. Pastels and muted tones are the signs of the bland, from our wardrobe to our palate and beyond. However there is a place for the crispness of white, the clean lines of a white plate showcasing a crafted menu; a white headband or shoe at one time signifying clarity of mind and body.

Punk style is embedded into many facets of our lives including our closet and our pantry. It manages to be a format for individual distinction and community building which makes for great dinner conversation.

The tattered clothes of punk, often imperfect on purpose, are allowed to be emboldened by their shreds from experience. The ripped fishnets and stained hoodie are perfectly thought out, even if thrown on, because the pieces are all part of a wardrobe of consciousness. The best food has great intentions and isn't belabored to the point of not letting it shine on its own. It is about intention with a willingness to be flexible in the result and its interpretation. Accents or garnish adds variety and personalization. Accessories are the little details.

For this section: very fashionable groups, sexy groups, songs that are cool for no reason, and songs about consumerism. Because there's nothing more punk than contradicting yourself!

1 - X RAY SPEX **"ARTIFICIAL"** *(Yes, them again!)*

2 - HUGGY BEAR **"HER JAZZ"**

3 - VIRGIN PRUNES **"PAGAN LOVE SONG"**

4 - SPECIMEN **"KISS KISS BANG BANG"** *(They looked like they crawled out of a pile of very fashionable garbage.)*

5 - FUZZBOX **"RULES AND REGULATIONS"**

6 - SIGUE SIGUE SPUTNIK **"SHE'S MY MAN"**

7 - JAPAN **"TRANSMISSION"** *(Doesn't David Sylvian look great!?)*

8 - UK DECAY **"DECADENCE"**

9 - THE SAINTS **"KNOW YOUR PRODUCT"**

10 - GENERATION X **"WILD YOUTH"**

11 - CHRISMA **"BLACK SILK STOCKING"** *(hot Italian)*

12 - GWAR **"I'M IN LOVE WITH A DEAD DOG"** *(This fabulous molten green dong from Diane von Thirstnforsperm matches perfectly with Christian di Whore puss and blood rouge bellybutton lipstick.)*

13 - UNDERTONES **"TEENAGE KICKS"**

14 - CITIZEN FISH **"PANIC IN THE SUPERMARKET"**

15 - THE ENEMY **"TRENDY VIOLENCE"**

16 - MINOR THREAT **"CASHING IN"**

17 - JAYNE COUNTY **"MAN ENOUGH TO BE A WOMAN"** *(Gotta look good.)*

18 - REFUSED **"THE SHAPE OF PUNK TO COME"** *(If you don't think this is stylized, you're nuts.)*

19 - BETTY DAVIS **"THEY SAY I'M DIFFERENT"**

20 - NEW YORK DOLLS **"JETBOY"**

21 - ELTON MOTELLO **"JET BOY JET GIRL"**

22 - THE TUBES **"WHITE PUNKS ON DOPE"**

FISHNET TARTS (OR TARTS IN FISHNETS!)

Girls, boys, and everyone in between *(and side to side)* love fishnets. They make everything sexier—or something like that! Showing that you don't care what anyone else thinks about your sexuality, and then putting it *in your own face* is what we are all about. Wooooooo! Sexy stuff. You need...

A PIE CRUST BATCH, WITH POMEGRANATE OR OTHER RED JUICE FOR THE LIQUID, INSTEAD OF WATER OR VODKA *(Unless it's red or pink vodka.)*
1/2 C. STRAWBERRIES
2 C. COCONUT CREAM
1/2 C. COCONUT FLOUR
PINCH OF SALT TO TASTE
1/3 C. SUGAR
4 OZ. BITTWERSWEET CHOCOLATE
1/4 C. BLACKBERRY JAM
2 TSP. CHOCOLATE MILK
1/2 TSP. VANILLA

Roll out pie crust and place in greased pie pan. Blend strawberries, coconut cream, coconut flour, sugar, and a bit of salt. Spoon into pie crust. Bake at 425 for 10 minutes, then drop heat to 375 and bake for another 15-20 or until crust is done/pinked *(AKA browned!)*. Cool/chill. While that cools, melt chocolate with jam and chocolate milk. Remove from heat and stir in vanilla. Allow to cool so that it can still be drizzled but holds its place alright. Now, of course you will drizzle your little heart out onto this pie in a fishnet pattern. This whole affair can be done in smaller servings—in ramekins or little tart pans. The baking times will be shorter. If you happen to have leg-shaped pans well, even better!

BRIGHT GREEN TOMATOES EEEK!

2 C. SLICED GREEN TOMATOES
1/2 C. GROUND PUMPKIN SEEDS
SALT TO TASTE
1/2 C. TOMATILLOS
2 OR 3 TSP. LIME JUICE
1 CHOPPED SEEDED ANAHEIM PEPPER
A FEW TSP. CHOPPED CILANTRO AND SCALLIONS
2 MINCED GARLIC CLOVES
GREEN CURRY POWDER TO TASTE
OIL FOR SAUTÉ, PLUS A LITTLE FOR SAUCE
1 TSP. KELP, SPIRULINA, OR SEAWEED POWDER
(something reallllly green!)
OPTIONAL: PEELED KIWI FRUIT *can be an interesting addition to this sauce*

Mix seaweed powder, ground pumpkin seeds, some salt, and green curry powder. Coat the tomatoes in this and fry, turning once, until cooked on both sides. Meanwhile, purée the other stuff and adjust the seasonings. Keep the sauce raw, since tomatillos will turn brown when cooked. Serve with the fried tomatoes.

A TRIO OF FLASHY DIPS
(SOUNDS LIKE A BAND I ONCE KNEW...)

-PURPLE-

1 C. COOKED PURPLE YAM
1/3 C. CHOPPED ROASTED/COOKED BEET
2 TSP. RED WINE VINEGAR
1/2 TSP. SUMAC POWDER
1 TSP. SMOKED PAPRIKA
1/3 C. RED ONION
A LITTLE PLUM VINEGAR (UMEBOSHI!)
SOME MINCED OR POWDERED GINGER
RED SALT (OR PLAIN) TO TASTE
LIQUID IF NEEDED (RED OR PURPLE OF COURSE!)

(deep, smoky, woody)

-YELLOW-

1 C. COOKED YELLOW STRING BEANS OR COOKED
CANARY BEANS
1/2 C. YELLOW BELL PEPPER
1/2 C. YELLOW TOMATO (BEST IF YOU SPLIT AND
ROAST THEM FOR A LITTLE WHILE)
1 TSP. TURMERIC
3 CLOVES GARLIC
2 OR MORE TSP. LEMON JUICE
1/3 C. CHOPPED MANGO

(light, fruity, vegetal)

-GREEN-

2 PITTED/PEELED, CHOPPED AVOCADOS
1/3 C. CHOPPED PARSLEY
1/2 C. FRESH PEAS
1/4 C. PITTED GREEN OLIVES (NO PIMENTO)
1/4 C. PISTACHIO OIL OR EXTRA VIRGIN
OLIVE OIL
4 CHOPPED SCALLIONS
LIME JUICE, SALT, AND WHITE PEPPER TO
TASTE
JALAPENO, AS YOU LIKE

(spicy, limey, rich)

Instructions are the same, blend each one until smooth *(or leave a bit of chunkiness if you prefer)*. Serve garishly garnished in inappropriate vessels.

SEAWEED LIBERTY SPIKES

SEVERAL NORI SHEETS
TAMARI *(to taste)*
try **GROUND BLACK SESAME,**
GARLIC POWDER, BLACK PEPPER *and a little*
WASABI POWDER, *maybe some* **SWEETENER**
SEVERAL TSP. MUSHROOM BROTH
1 TSP. SESAME OIL

Mix tamari, oil, spice mix, and broth together. Brush onto nori sheets. Roll each one up diagonally into a long, twisty cone, or spike shape *(or ropes)*. Either fry them in oil until crispy or place on a baking sheet, brush thoroughly, and bake at 325 for 15 or so, turning once. Keep an eye on them, as they can burn somewhat easily. When crispy, take them out—it won't take very long. They can be arranged at table in a bowl like a frightwig if you make enough of them.

LEOPARD MEZZA

Pretty simple for something pretty cute. Purée
SWEET POTATOES with **LIME JUICE, 1 GARLIC**
CLOVE, GINGER, COUPLE TSP. OLIVE OIL,
AND SALT TO TASTE. Set aside. Purée **WHITE BEANS,**
CASHEW MILK, SALT, 2 GARLIC CLOVES, 1 OR 2
TSP.
OLIVE OIL, AND LEMON JUICE TO TASTE.

SAFETY ORANGE DELIGHT

Pay attention to the texture of this one, you should be able to spoon it onto something in a pattern but it can't be so runny that it goes all over the place. Add more beans or liquid as the case may be. Or if you have a pastry bag you can make it a more frosting-like texture and pipe it on. Cooked potato can also be an enjoyable addition to it. This is fun to concoct—spread some of the sweet potato around on a plate or in a bowl. Now create a feral pattern out of the bean spread and the olives and string beans; making it look like a leopard's atttractive coat. Or cheetah. Or ocelot. Essentially you have all of the components, it's up to you to make it interesting. Seaweed may also be used to do up some tricky patterns. Serve with pita and crudites.

This is a good dish with carrots as the main ingredient. If you add reds/pinks to the mix it will become more strange and garishly orange, so things like beet juice and chili sauce can be thrown in there at your discretion to make it look crazier, just do it a dash at a time. One of my favorite shirts to wear was bright yellow with a bright orange "X" on it. When worn with purple cords, I found this to be a delightful outfit. Lord help us, I'm sure it was ugly as sin. Serve this crazy crap with pita or crackers and crudites.

Coarsely chop yam, carrot and halve the habanero (seed it) and orange tomatoes. Coat with some oil, salt and pepper and roast at 400 for 30 minutes. Cool down and purée with the other ingredients to create a bright dip. Adding a little pink or red to it makes it look crazier which is why the beet juice is involved and some chili sauce not a bad idea as well. Did I say that already? Tough!

ADJUST SEASONINGS TO TASTE.
ORANGE BELL PEPPER
2 TSP. GRATED FRESH TURMERIC ROOT
2 CARROTS
A LITTLE BEET JUICE *(about a teaspoon, maybe more)*
1 HABANERO
2 PEELED GARLIC CLOVES
A FEW TBSP. OLIVE OIL
1/4 C. LEMON JUICE
SALT AND WHITE PEPPER TO TASTE.
2 ORANGE TOMATOES
1 PEELED GARNET YAM

SECRET INGREDIENT: A PACKET
OF EMERGEN-C OR OTHER FRUITY
VITAMIN C THING *(it makes it crazy
good, trust me, punks always have these lying around for hangovers!)*

BLACK AND SILVER WRISTBAND BAR

The wristband is part of the standard uniform, nothing like the ol' black and silver to jazz up the place.

8 OZ. DARK CHOCOLATE
1/2 TSP. ANISE/LICORICE OR ALMOND FLAVORING
1/2 TSP. VANILLA
2 TSP. CHOCOLATE SOY MILK OR OTHER
1 TSP. OIL, COCONUT OIL OR MARGARINE-Y SUBSTANCE
PINCH OF SALT TO TASTE
LICORICE OR CHOCOLATE DROPS *(Like kiss-shaped.)*
SILVER FOOD PAINT *(Of course!)*
you can add **CHOPPED NUTS,** *just toast them first*

Set the candy drops on wax paper and spray or paint them silver with your food paint. Set aside to dry.

Melt the chocolate with soy milk and oil in a double boiler. Remove from heat and stir in anise, vanilla, and salt.

Pour into bar-shaped candy molds *(you can make them yourself if need be, using plastic trays)* and start to cool.

Before they are completely solid, stud attractively with your silver kissies.

Voila. Everyone will be so jealous.

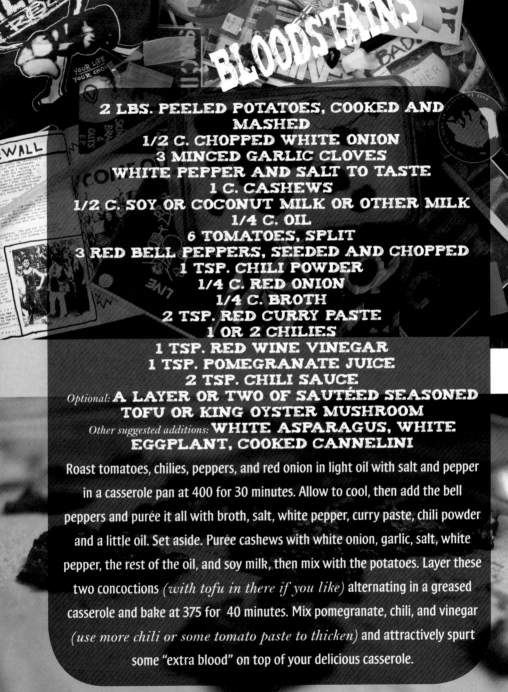

2 LBS. PEELED POTATOES, COOKED AND
MASHED
1/2 C. CHOPPED WHITE ONION
3 MINCED GARLIC CLOVES
WHITE PEPPER AND SALT TO TASTE
1 C. CASHEWS
1/2 C. SOY OR COCONUT MILK OR OTHER MILK
1/4 C. OIL
6 TOMATOES, SPLIT
3 RED BELL PEPPERS, SEEDED AND CHOPPED
1 TSP. CHILI POWDER
1/4 C. RED ONION
1/4 C. BROTH
2 TSP. RED CURRY PASTE
1 OR 2 CHILIES
1 TSP. RED WINE VINEGAR
1 TSP. POMEGRANATE JUICE
2 TSP. CHILI SAUCE
Optional: **A LAYER OR TWO OF SAUTÉED SEASONED
TOFU OR KING OYSTER MUSHROOM**
Other suggested additions: **WHITE ASPARAGUS, WHITE
EGGPLANT, COOKED CANNELINI**

Roast tomatoes, chilies, peppers, and red onion in light oil with salt and pepper
in a casserole pan at 400 for 30 minutes. Allow to cool, then add the bell
peppers and purée it all with broth, salt, white pepper, curry paste, chili powder
and a little oil. Set aside. Purée cashews with white onion, garlic, salt, white
pepper, the rest of the oil, and soy milk, then mix with the potatoes. Layer these
two concoctions *(with tofu in there if you like)* alternating in a greased
casserole and bake at 375 for 40 minutes. Mix pomegranate, chili, and vinegar
(use more chili or some tomato paste to thicken) and attractively spurt
some "extra blood" on top of your delicious casserole.

5.

CRUNCHY, SWEATY, SHAKY, SMELLY

We punks love to argue
about what kind of punk is what.
That's not trash, that's crust.
They're not pop punk they're power punk.
It's not art wave it's lesbian!
And so forth.

We're obsessed with the minutiae and minor
differences. Can't we all just get along?

No, we can't! Each genre has its own specific sounds,
looks, and vibes. And you can't convince a punk to
like shit they just don't like.

Now imagine telling this to Helen Keller. The only
way to explain it properly would be through a touch
and feel session; an exploration of genres through
texture, smell, and composition. And that's what
we have here. Because, hell, food has a story
to tell and it's better than words!
Or maybe even music!

Crunchy, Sweaty, Shaky, Smelly

"THE REAL DEAL IS NOT TOO HARD TO SPOT IN APPAREL OR FOOD." – ROCKSWORTH SEXINGTON

"I WOULD NEVER EAT THAT FUCKING VEGAN SHIT!!!! SOOOO, WHAT IS THIS I'M EATING???"- JULIE LARY (LEVIATHAN/ FEMETARY/ SPECIAL FRIEND)

by Stiff Leggings

Taste and smell also help to guide. Let's face it, some punk rock really stinks, or leaves a foul, grimey taste in your mouth. Perhaps we should just smear coffee grounds all over everything. It's easy to play around with these aspects of flavor, odors, and cooking in the context of sound—overly sweet, hot, fruity, dirty, crisp, bitter, or sour. Or too long and slow. Haha! Come up with your own interpretations.

We have some interesting color schemes here as well. It's all a rich tapestry. Whether informed with pleasant, abrasive, vivid, confrontational, or melancholy tastes, colors, smells and textures—these dishes can help inspire us to finally get to the bottom of what it is about sound that makes us crap our pants.

This chapter has some art to it, so I thought the playlist shouldn't have any. Also, the pop punk cupcake is the best thing in this chapter, so it's all pop punk. Sort of.

1 - DESCENDENTS "BIKEAGE"
2 - THE FASTBACKS "IN THE SUMMER"
(Optimistic, yup, that's me!)
3 - CUB "GO FISH"
4 - REDD KROSS "PLAY MY SONG"
5 - BIG DRILL CAR "LES COCHONS SANS POILS"
6 - GUTTERMOUTH "MR. BARBEQUE" *(This has a lot to do with the book.)*
7 - GREEN DAY "DRY ICE"
8 - CRIMPSHRINE "BUTTERFLIES"
9 - ANGRY SAMOANS "RIGHT SIDE OF MY MIND"
10 - THE DICKIES "ROSEMARY"
11 - THE HI-FIVES "I'D BE SO PLEASED"
12 - SYCAMORE SMITH "SHAN-TAN-TITTY-TOWN" *(Try getting this one out of your head.)*
13 - J CHURCH "FOREIGN FILMS" *(It's hard not to get sentimental when one like this comes on.)*
14 - LEMONHEADS "HATE YOUR FRIENDS"
15 - COFFIN BREAK "KILL THE PRESIDENT"
16 - GHOST MICE "I'LL BE HAPPY"
17 - KENT 3 "THE DUKE OF FEDERAL WAY"
18 - WAVVES "SAIL TO THE SUN"
19 - MR. T EXPERIENCE "21"
20 - TOY DOLLS "DIG THAT GROOVE BABY"
(Might as well go out with a bang.)

FILTHY FRUIT QUEERCORE RING

A variety of Carmen Miranda-oriented fruits with different textures best epitomize the eclectic sounds of the movement.

1 C. CHOPPED PINEAPPLE
1 C. CHOPPED BANANA
1/4 C. POMEGRANATE SEEDS
1/2 C. PEELED, SEEDED, DICED CUCUMBER
(surprise)
1 C. CHOPPED APRICOTS AND/OR PLUMS
1/2 C. DICED GRANNY SMITH APPLE
1 C. CHOPPED VEGAN MARSHMALLOWS
1/3 C. RAW CACAO POWDER WITH A LITTLE SUGAR
1 TSP. LEMON JUICE
A HALF CUP OF CHOPPED TOASTED HAZELNUTS
1/2 C. TOASTED COCONUT
A FEW PINCHES SALT
1 TSP. VANILLA
1/2 TSP. POPPY SEEDS

This is basically ambrosia. As you can see, even though there is a bit of "vanilla" there is also "caca." The raw cacao is fatty, dirty, and gritty. That's what we like! Adjust seasonings to taste *(I know you will!)*. That about covers it. This has a whole troop of textures in one place.

Popcorn is crunchy. Fake crunchy! Like styrofoam. Like pop punk, it ain't so tough. The sticky fruit pieces reinforce that—hey, it's...

POP PUNK RAINBOW POPCORN PUNCH CUPCAKES

1 1/2 C. FLOUR
1 C. SUGAR
2 TSP. BAKING POWDER
2/3 C. COCONUT MILK
1/3 C. OIL
1 TSP VANILLA
1 TSP. ORANGE FLAVOR
1 TSP. LEMON FLAVOR
FOOD COLORING *(Three kinds.)*
POPCORN
CANDIED FRUIT
A LITTLE VEGAN CREAM CHEESE *(Because, why not?!)*
POWDERED SUGAR
LEMON JUICE
ORANGE JUICE
RASPBERRY, STRAWBERRY, OR BLUEBERRY JAM

Mix flour, sugar, and baking powder. Set aside. Mix together vanilla, oil, and coconut milk, and blend with the dry ingredients. Separate into three bowls, add food colorings and flavorings accordingly. Line a muffin or cupcake pan. Spoon batter in layers or a trio of globs, alternating colors/flavors. You can get really elaborate with that if you like. Include some minced fruit candy in there. Bake at 350 for 20-25 or until cooked throughout. Cool and frost using:

1 C. POWDERED SUGAR
A FEW TSP. FRUIT JUICES
FOOD COLORING
SEVERAL TSP. VEGAN CREAM CHEESE
SEVERAL TSP. MARGARINE

Mix these together, using different combinations of colorings and flavorings. Decorate your cupcakes attractively. Next, melt 1/2 C. sugar in 1/4 C. oil or margarine. Remove from heat, separate into a few bowls, and add food colorings. Toss this concoction in with your popcorns. Decorate the cupcakes with this, candied fruit, and sprinkles, if you have them around. Doesn't that just make ya happy?! If you have a pastry bag around, fill the cupcakes with jam before frosting.

BOUNCY BLACK AND WHITE SKA PIE

1 1/4 C. SIFTED FLOUR
1 TSP. SUGAR
SALT
1/2 C. MARGARINE OR COCONUT OIL
SEVERAL TSP. COLD WATER
SEVERAL TSP. COCOA POWDER

Mix together flour, sugar, and salt. Add margarine to make crumbs, then water gradually to make dough. Split dough and add cocoa powder to one half. Now begin rolling these out on a floured board, tearing pieces off and overlapping them, black and white. Now roll the whole thing out and press into a greased 10" pie or tart pan. Maybe you can make it look like a zebra.

1 C. COCONUT
1/3 C. COCONUT MILK
1/4 C. SUGAR
1/4 C. FLOUR
2 TSP. OIL OR MARGARINE
SALT TO TASTE

Mix this concoction together. Set aside.

1/3 C. COCOA POWDER
1/2 C. CHOCOLATE CHIPS
1/2 C. CHOCOLATE SOYMILK
1/4 C. FLOUR
1/2 C. BROWN SUGAR
1 TSP. VANILLA
SALT TO TASTE
2 TSP. OIL/MARGARINE

Mix this together. Now place the black goop and the white goop alternatingly into the pie crust. It won't exactly be a checkerboard.

This will be a fateful experiment—either it will largely hold its shape (you can assist by making sure your goop is fairly solid), or perhaps meld together. Only fate can decide.

Bake at 425 for 10 minutes, then lower heat to 375 and bake for 15-20 minutes more. Cool on a wire rack.

Decorate with black and white chocolate chips and your favorite "whipped topping" recipe. Half plain, and the other half with some cocoa powder and espresso powder mixed in.

Ner ner ner ner ner ner ner ner ner ner ner ner ner

ner ner ner ner—that was to a ska tune. I think it's "Too Much Pressure."

Now this just tastes *filthy*.

SKRAKKY CRUST PUNK BRICKLE

BLACK CRACKERS *(use your imagination)*
1/2 C. CHOPPED DARK CHOCOLATE
1/4 C. DARK CORN SYRUP
1/4 C. GROUND BLACK SESAME SEEDS
1/2 C. DARK BROWN SUGAR
1 TSP. COFFEE POWDER
2 TSP. BLACK MARGARINE *(Haha! Plain margarine is fine.)*
PIECES OF CHOPPED UP BLACK CANDY

Melt brown sugar and corn syrup with margarine, and heat to a gurgly simmer for several minutes. Add everything but the candy and crackers, stir. Remove from heat. With tongs or whatever, dip crackers in this stuff and then in the crushed up candy. Set aside somewhere they won't stick, then wait for them to harden.

It amuses me to rep emo with an alcoholic drink.
Just look at 'em all now...or then!

EMO SOUR LEMON DROP

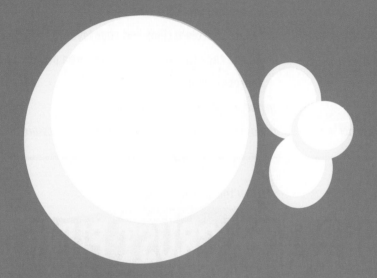

3 PARTS VODKA
1 PART LIMONCELLO
1 PART LEMON JUICE
1 PART TRIPLE SEC
ICE
LEMON SLICE
LEMON CANDIES OR SOURS

Don't bother with the sugar rim, boohoohoo!!
Shake vodka, limoncello, lemon juice, and Triple Sec with ice. Strain into cocktail glasses and serve with a lemon slice. The limoncello helps with that metrosexual, eurofaggish feel of some of the more modern emo styles, and frankly, some of the old as well. Americans just shouldn't be that hapless.

And just to get laid too. How hard is that?!

ART/NOISE CORE PERFORMANCE ART DECONSTRUCTED SUSHI

Uh-oh... when music is overly obtuse or "artistic" and pretentious there is only one thing to do... make sushi!!

**ROASTED NORI SHEETS
DAIKON
CARROT
RED BELL PEPPER
AVOCADO
GINGER
NATTO AND DURIAN
A DRAGONFRUIT
RICE VINEGAR
SALT
COOKED SUSHI RICE
TOASTED SESAME SEEDS
PLUM VINEGAR
WASABI
LIME JUICE
A FRYING PAN**

Julienne the daikon, carrot, bell pepper, ginger, and slice the avocado. Sprinkle variously with lime juice and the vinegars and a little salt.

Place them on a tray and leave the room.

In the next room place the nori sheets on the floor.

Go to the next room, but on your way there hang the frying pan in the doorway and turn the lights out.

In the next room hide the durian behind the couch.

Go to the foyer. Place the dragonfruit on a pedestal here with a spotlight on it.

Now go out on the porch and mix rice with sesame seeds and some seasonings.

Mix the natto with wasabi.

Cover yourself in a shroud.

As your guests arrive, feed them the spicy natto with one hand while "eating" the rice through the cloth of your shroud with the other.

I think I saw this band once.

NO REALLY THO', HERE'S SOME DECONSTRUCTED SUSHI

1/2 C. WAKAME, RECONSTITUTED
1 OR 2 SHEETS SUSHI NORI
1 TSP. BLACK SESAME SEEDS
1 TSP. WHITE SESAME SEEDS, TOASTED
1/4 C. KIMCHEE
1 C. COOKED BLACK RICE
2 TBSP. CHOPPED WATER CHESTNUTS
1 TBSP. PREPARED WASABI
A FEW SLICES PICKLED GINGER
2 AVOCADOS, PITTED AND HALVED
DRY SESAME SHEET *(you know, one of those dry inedible frisbees with the sesame seeds embedded in it)*
1 TBSP. RICE VINEGAR
SALT TO TASTE
A LITTLE SESAME OIL

Cut wakame into thin short strips and mix with both sesame seeds, salt and a little rice vinegar and sesame oil to taste. Set aside.

Gently wet the nori sheets and stick to the outside of the avocado halves and trim, to mimic the skin.

Cook the sesame cracker in microwave until it puffs up *(it shouldn't take long, just keep an eye on it)* set aside. Mix kimchee, rice, rice vinegar, salt water chestnuts, and a little wasabi together. Form into 4 balls and place in the avocado halves on small black plates. Next, balance a piece of crispy sesame cracker on top of each rice ball.

Then top with a dollop of the wakame mixture.

Final touch: a little wasabi on top.

ABRASIVE AND SWEET AND SOUR RIOT GRRRL BITES

To razorblades add... just kidding! I'm a fan of the stuff, having been an Oly alumnus. Nonetheless, sticks and sweets and rocks and treats... that's what we're all made of.

1/2 C. CHOPPED TOASTED HAZELNUTS
1/2 C. CHOPPED TOASTED ALMONDS
2 TSP. GRATED LEMON PEEL
1 C. CHOCOLATE CHIPS
1 TSP. OIL
1/2 TSP. HOT CHILI POWDER
1/2 TSP. POWDERED GINGER
1/2 TSP. LEMON FLAVORING
1/2 TSP. GROUND LEMONGRASS

Melt the chocolate chips. Add the rest and pour into candy molds. Allow to cool. These are pretty good. It is largely the flavors that represent. White chocolate would be more appropriate! Hahaha!

"I USED TO THINK ALL VEGAN DESERTS
WERE NOT WORTH MY TIME OF DAY AND
THEN I MET JOSHUA."
- CATHY DE LA CRUZ
(FILMMAKER/WRITER/DJ OMG)

MOLASSES GEL SLUDGEY DOOMCORE

Oh you know, nobody likes molasses. It is slow and tastes burnt. And this sludgy doom post metal/punk burnout slow music, you really need to be stoned to listen to it. The mason jar is appropriate because many sludgy, slow bands come from the south or some other "down home" place. They're all sittin' there on the porch in their overalls and no shirt or shoes, feet sitting in a bucket of molasses, bigass beard, smoking dope in a corncob pipe. What's punk about that? Nothing, absolutely nothing. Get caught in a mush!

PREPARE A BATCH OF VEGAN JELL-O BUT ADD MOLASSES AS PART OF THE LIQUID AND COFFEE AS THE REST.

You will also need some
-VEGAN WHIPPED CREAM CONCOCTION-
1 C. COCONUT CREAM *mixed with*
2 TSP. POWDERED SUGAR
1 T. POWDERED COCOA OR MELTED CHOCOLATE
1 TSP. ESPRESSO POWDER *and spoon that on top.*

The coffee represents how these stoned heshers like to come to life and toss me across the room from time to time.

Or you can make the gel yourself without using pre-packaged concoctions:
2 C. LIQUID, *heated to a boil*
MIX WITH 1 TSP. AGAR

Take out half a cup of liquid and whisk in
1 TBSP. CORNSTARCH

Add it back to the agar liquid and stir.

Chill until somewhat congealed

* for this recipe I would go with 1 2/3 C. coffee and 1/3 C. molasses for the liquid concoction

DURIAN SOUP WITH SEAWEED CRISPS

You know who smells or should smell bad? Punks. You know what else smells? Durian. The soup epitomizes the essence of a stinky, self-righteous punk rocker. Here, it's raw as well. Just to be extra high on the ol' horse! And at long last, you now know something to do with durian. Sometimes fruit just can't take a shower on the long barge journey across the sea, just like sometimes a punk rocker can't take a shower on the long journey through life! I've smelled really bad before. And recently. There's no shame in it.

1 1/2 C. CHOPPED DURIAN
1 C. COCONUT MILK
1 C. COCONUT CREAM OR MEAT
1/4 C. CHOPPED THAI BASIL
1 TBSP. RICE VINEGAR
1 TSP. CHOPPED GALANGAL
1 TSP. MINCED LEMONGRASS
TAMARI OR SALT TO TASTE
2 TSP. CURRY POWDER
1 SMALL MINCED CHILI, SEEDED
2 PEELED GARLIC CLOVES
2 TBSP. MINCED CILANTRO
CARROT, SHREDDED
SCALLIONS, MINCED FOR GARNISH
LIME

** To make sweet and turn into an ice cream instead:
omit tamari and garlic, add 1/3 to 1/2 C. sugar, purée and freeze,
stirring occasionally. The other ingredients are up to you whether to
include or leave out, to me they all work in there.*

Take 1 C. of the durian and blend with coconut milk, cream, tamari or salt, curry, galangal, lemongrass, garlic, chili most of the basil and vinegar. Chill. Season to taste. Serve with rest of the chopped durian, shredded carrot, lime wedges, scallion and cilantro. You really don't haaaave to chill it, if you don't want to.

TO MAKE SEAWEED CRISPS:

Baste sheets of nori with a little tamari and sesame oil, dip/dredge in sesame seeds and bake at 350 on a sheet, turning at least once, for 7-12 minutes or until "re-encrispened" *(after becoming a lil soggy with the basting).* It might be a good idea to have parchment on your baking sheet.

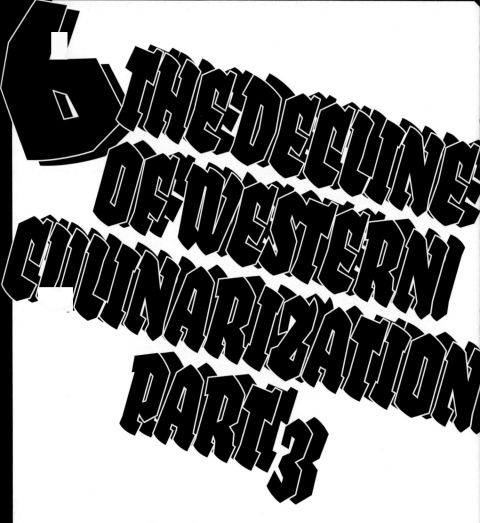

6 THE DECLINE OF WESTERN CULINARIZATION PART 3

Is that even a word?

"Um... don't try'n tell me whut to do." Crust punks, the wuvvable raconteurs of any respectable punk scene have their own innovative methods of dealing with things. Any self-respecting crusty is a one-punk mobile kitchen, with many means at their disposable. And now you, their hosts, will understand what to do with all of the gifts of dumpstered bread and ancient produce they left you as "thanks" for "letting" them crash for those two or three or four or five months on your couch. That's if they didn't burn your house down trying to make s'mores.

The Decline of Western Culinarization

by Eric Ingrate

Crusties are the future. Not so much an end point, but a vision of what we have to expect in that brief, terrifying moment when everything stops. Sure, they are an image of the past—the recalled shiver of Amebix living in the cold opiate haze of squats in southern England, the image of angry rioters in Tompkins Square Park, and the echo of smashing glass in Eugene or Seattle. But at the same moment, they are recalling our collective past of dodgey hygiene, scarce money, and frequent inebriation; they are prefiguring a world where we have substantively broke with western standards of beauty and cleanliness while forsaking capitalism to dance a bacchanal on the ruins of society. Don't get me wrong, I am not trying to say that the crusties have it all figured out, or that they are some sort of model that we should actively aspire to become, but rather they are a glimpse of where we all might soon find ourselves; given peak oil, late-stage capitalism, and the increasing social tensions endemic to mass consumer culture.

That is their beauty—are crusties anti-consumer? No! They consume, and consume, and consume (and vomit, and vomit, and vomit). The critical question is not "do they consume?" but what do they consume? Do they walk in the front door of Noah's Bagels to purchase a fresh-this-morning everything bagel with lox, or (perhaps) non-dairy cream cheese? NO! The crusty knows that this is a ruse, a clever way to keep the rest of us in line, complacent. Paying for our food, when the same bounty can be found out back in the dumpster for nothing. Fresh? Not exactly. Consider them slightly preserved. That grey looking, half-eaten tub of (shall we say?) ripe lox? One could choose to look at it as the index question that sorts the weak-stomached walking dead from the survivors who will feast on civilization's waste. Or, perhaps one could look at that lox as another reason to go vegan...Whatever the case, when the lights go out, and the road warrior shit starts to go down, count me with the crusties. Eating stale bagels toasted on the flames of a burning cop car.

We jumped off the train at the edge of town. It was well after dark. After we found a small field and stashed our packs, we headed towards the lights of a shopping complex and identified our targets. While Ramona headed to the grocery to Crimethinc an avocado and a tomato, I made my way to the back of the bagel shoppe and watched as the closing employee walked back in the door. I had timed this perfectly! In the mind of this low-wage worker he had taken out the trash but to this road-weary and unwashed anarcho-punk, he had merely restocked my large green coffer with treasure.

Swiftly, I hopped the fence enclosing the dumpster and found it—locked! The bastard capitalists and their wage-slave lackeys were trying to wage their class war upon me, but this was a battle that I would win. I produced my small tube of superglue and filled the padlock's keyhole with the sticky and quick-bonding fluid. In the same motion, I grasped my multitool and went to work dismantling the hinges, flipping the lid of this container of stale goodness off the opposite way. This would teach them to mess with the international punk underground! The next day, as we hitched out of Madison in the rain, our bellies were full and the flames of our discontent were freshly fueled by the only thing that mattered—stolen produce and dumpstered bagels. We knew that the future held limitless and unknown possibilities. A red sportscar pulled off the road, the older man inside yelling at someone on his cell phone gestured for us to get in.

We sped off on the highway west, unsure of our destination, but ready for adventure. Fashion and food continues to be shaped by cultural needs and each region, economic up and down swing, and influential voice present new ideas to resonate loudly, and hopefully shake our insides like a crowded basement show.

So is this music all crust, you may ask? Much of it is but, not everything. It's just some of the shit that they like. A lot of standards, like the crusty version of the Lawrence Welk Show.

1 - AMEBIX "LARGACTYL" *(If this is a bird it must be really big and scary and dirty.)*

2 - DESTROY "TOTAL FUCKING CHAOS"

3 - ANTISCHISM "PATH OF DESTRUCTION"

4 - EXCREMENT OF WAR "SHIT SOCIETY" *(They mean the one YOU live in!)*

5 - DIRT "OBJECT REFUSE REJECT ABUSE"

6 - NAUSEA "TECH NO LOGIC KILL" *(I see what ya did there.)*

7 - HELLBASTARD "HEADING FOR INTERNAL DARKNESS"

8 - ISKRA "ACCEPTANCE NOT TOLERANCE" *(This band is pretty much the crust sound.)*

9 - CORRUPTED "LA VICTIMA ES TU MISMO"

10 - EXTREME NOISE TERROR "FUCKED UP SYSTEM"

11 - HIS HERO IS GONE "LIKE WEEDS"

12 - TOTALITAR "KLASS INTE RAS" *(So true.)*

13 - ANTI CIMEX "WAVE OF FEAR"

14 - DYSTOPIA "SLEEP"

15 - MISERY "FILTH OF MANKIND"

16 - ELECTRO HIPPIES "SHEEP" *(They mean YOU!)*

17 - CRISIS REBIRTH "KLEPTOCRACY" *(Because they're like stealing from ya man!)*

18 - DISFEAR "GET IT OFF"

19 - ANTISECT "RESIST AND EXIST"

20 - DOOM "POLICE BASTARD" *(It is a rule to have at least one song about cops.)*

OLD DUMPSTERED BAGEL RAREBIT AND 40 OZ. MIMOSA

6 BAGELS, SPLIT, AND TOASTED
OIL, SALT, AND PEPPER TO TASTE
1 SMALL, THINLY SLICED RED ONION

-TOMATO SAUCE-
3 CLOVES GARLIC
2 C. TOMATOES, CHOPPED, SEEDED, AND DRAINED
2 RED BELL PEPPERS, SEEDED, AND PREFERABLY ROASTED AND CHOPPED
HERBS *(a handful, of thyme, chervil, oregano, chives etc.)*
1 TSP. LEMON JUICE
SALT AND PEPPER
1/2 C. BEER
A LITTLE THICKENER *such as some sort of flour may be added, only a few Tsp. if any*

-CHEEZY SAUCE-
1/2 C. CASHEWS
1/4 C. SESAME SEEDS
2 TSP. PREPARED MUSTARD
SALT AND WHITE PEPPER
COUPLE TSP. TO 1/4 C. OIL
2 OR 3 TSP. WHITE BALSAMIC VINEGAR
OR LEMON JUICE *(more if you want)*
1/2 C. COOKED WHITE BEANS
1/4 C. DICED ONION
TURMERIC OR CURRY POWDER TO TASTE
1 C. SOME TYPE OF "MILK" OR BROTH-
UNSWEETENED OF COURSE!
PAPRIKA

Place the bagels in a greased pan with red onions. Salt and pepper to taste. Blend the **TOMATO SAUCE** ingredients together, season to taste and pour over the bagels. Bake at 400 for 20 minutes. Meanwhile blend your **CHEEZY SAUCE** ingredients together, adjust seasonings to taste. Pour over the bagel-tomato party. Sprinkle with paprika. Bake for another 20 minutes. Finish under the broiler if you like.

-40 OZ MIMOSA-

20 OZ. ORANGE JUICE
40 OZ. BEER
20 OZ. SPARKLING ORANGE BEVERAGE
(Can also be alcoholic. In fact, please do!)
ORANGE SLICES
CHILI ORANGE SALT

Makes two!

Do any orange-y beers come in a 40?! Well, if not, use a lighter beer with a lot of alcohol in it. Might I suggest malt liquor? For **CHILI ORANGE SALT:** grind dried orange peel and dried chili into a powder with some salt *(and maybe a little sugar)* Pour/layer however you deem fit into the biggest steins you can find, having of course salted the rims with that chili orange salt. Garnish with orange slices.

BEER CARAMEL POPCORN

HALF BOTTLE OF BEER
1/4 C. MARGARINE OR OIL
1 C. BROWN SUGAR
1/2 C. SOYMILK OR CREAMER *(or other- coconut for example)*
SALT TO TASTE
1 TSP. VANILLA
A PINCH OF NUTMEG
POPCORN
ROASTED PEANUTS, TOASTED PECANS, WALNUTS, OR HAZELNUTS

Heat beer in a saucepan and simmer for 5-10 minutes, reducing a bit. Next add the oil/margarine and allow to melt before adding the sugar. Cook for about 10 minutes, the sugar will get to a modest candy making phase. Do not turn up the burner too high. Add the rest of the ingredients and whisk together. Cook for a few minutes more then remove from heat. Add nuts if you're using them. Pop your popcorn and mix with the sauce and enjoy.

BAGEL FRENCH TOAST

3 OR 4 CINNAMON RAISIN BAGELS
1/2 C. FIRM TOFU
2 OR 3 TSP. MELTED MARGARINE OR COCONUT OIL
SALT TO TASTE
2 TSP. SUGAR OR AGAVE
1 TSP. NUTRITIONAL YEAST
1/4 C. FLOUR
1/2 TSP. BAKING POWDER
1/2 TSP. CINNAMON
1/4 TSP. NUTMEG
1/2 C. TO 1 C. SOYMILK, COCONUT MILK, OR NUT MILK (VANILLA IS FINE)
1 TSP. VANILLA (HALF FOR THE SOAK, HALF FOR THE COATING)
A LITTLE OIL TO COOK
BANANAS

Halve the bagels and toast them. Place in a casserole and pour a little soymilk and vanilla over them and let them soak it up. Blend the other ingredients until smooth. Use as much liquid as needed to make a pancake-like batter. Make sure it tastes pretty good. Dip the bagle halves in the mixture to coat and fry them in light oil, turning once, until browned on both sides. Syrup, jam, and almond butter make a killer combo to have with these. Add bananas.

CRUSTY CUPBOARD SPECIAL SURPRISE!

Well all of those trips to the food bank have left you with...

1 CAN GREEN BEANS
1 CAN CORN
1 CAN PUMPKIN
1 CAN CRANBERRY SAUCE

Fortunately, you also have:
A LITTLE OIL
SEVERAL CLOVES OF GARLIC
AN ONION
PAPRIKA
CURRY POWDER
CHILI SAUCE *(yes, sriracha comes to mind—I also think crusties like Cholula better than Tapatio because the wood knob seems more like "old Mexico" to them. But I can't prove it. I lived in Mexico. Tapatio is better!)*
SOME FLOUR AND
BAKING POWDER *(or a beer or 7-up or some similar shit at least)*
SALT

Let's see... Blend cranberry sauce with curry powder, a little diced onion, and hot sauce to taste. Set aside. Purée pumpkin and corn with half of the onion, garlic cloves, and a Tsp. or two of oil. Pour into a saucepan and add water, salt, some paprika, and curry powder to your desired thickness. Yes, you can and should use the corn liquid in place of water. Chili sauce to taste. Heat to just below boiling and simmer the bugger for 10 minutes or so, stirring here and there. Adjust seasonings. As you can see, so far you have soup and "chutney"...I guess. We're making fritters out of the green beans. Combine the green beans, and half of the green bean liquid with the rest of the onion, about a cup of flour *(more if need be)*, salt to taste and a tsp. of baking powder or a dash or two of beer. Fry in hot oil *(shallow is fine)*, turning once, until browned. Serve with soup and sauce. Of course, some delicious toasted bagels would be top notch with this.

OLD DUMPSTERED BAGEL (OR MUFFIN, EVEN WORSE!) BREAD PUDDING

**6 TO 8 OLD ASS BAGELS FROM THE DUMP
OR EQUIVALENT MUFFINAGE
1 CAN COCONUT MILK OR EQUIVALENT
SOY MILK
2 C. SOY MILK OR EQUIVALENT COCONUT
MILK
1/4 C. TAPIOCA FLOUR** *(crusties and tapioca, who knew?!)*
**2 BANANAS, MASHED
2 TSP. LEMON OR LIME JUICE
1/2 C. BROWN SUGAR** *(more to taste)*
**2 TSP. VANILLA
SALT TO TASTE
1/4 C. MARGARINE OR OIL OR COCONUT
OIL OR COCONUT MARGARINE
CINNAMON
LOTS AND LOTS OF CINNAMON
A PINCH OF NUTMEG**

For this, mix all but the bagels. Season deliciously to taste. Slice and toast the bagels. Crumble them into a greased casserole. Pour the rest over the tawwwwwwwwwwwp! Bake at 375 for 25 minutes. Sprinkle with some cinnamon, nutmeg, and a little sugar. Continue baking for another 15-20 minutes.

BEER AND UNCHEEZ SOUP WITH BAGEL CROUTONS FOR CRUSTY

1/4 C. OIL
2 TSP. PREPARED MUSTARD
1 C. DICED ONIONS
2 MINCED GARLIC CLOVES
1 C. DICED CAULIFLOWER
1 C. PEELED DICED POTATOES
1 C. DICED PARSNIPS
3 C. BROTH
1 C. BEER
1/2 C. CHOPPED TEMPEH "BACON"
2 TSP. MISO
1/4 C. NUTRITIONAL YEAST *(They love the stuff.)*
1/2 C. COOKED, MASHED WHITE BEANS *(I love the stuff.)*
SAUERKRAUT JUICE TO TASTE *(Kombucha or rejuvelac could also be entertaining right at the end.)*
SALT AND WHITE PEPPER TO TASTE

Sauté the vegetables in oil, with salt and white pepper, for three or four minutes. Add everything else except the beer and veggie bacon and cook, stirring occasionally, for 20 minutes. Meanwhile, sauté that veggie bacon until crispy. Set aside. Take a masher to the vegetables, and begin slowly adding beer and any other seasonings you feel necessary. More liquid, less liquid, whatever you like. Toast some bagel pieces on a baking sheet with a little oil, garlic powder, herbs, and salt on them to use for croutons.

Good garnishes: the tempeh bacon you just cooked, bagel croutons and chopped scallions *(surprise!)*.

COFFEE SAUCE FOR EVERYTHING

Spill this on your clothes to be an extra dirtbag!

1 C. SLICED MUSHROOMS *(something expensive, but stolen, but not really stolen. We would never suggest you steal anything!)*

1/2 C. MINCED ONION
2 TSP. OIL
1 C. RED WINE
1 C. BROTH
1 1/2 C. COFFEE
1 TSP. MINCED SAGE LEAVES
1 TSP. BROWN SUGAR
1 TSP. CORNSTARCH MIXED WITH 1/4 C. BROTH OR COFFEE
SALT AND PEPPER TO TASTE
2 MINCED GARLIC CLOVES

Whatever. Mix this shit together and simmer, stirring for 15 minutes or until it thickens a bit. If you don't have time for this, you're a busy punk!

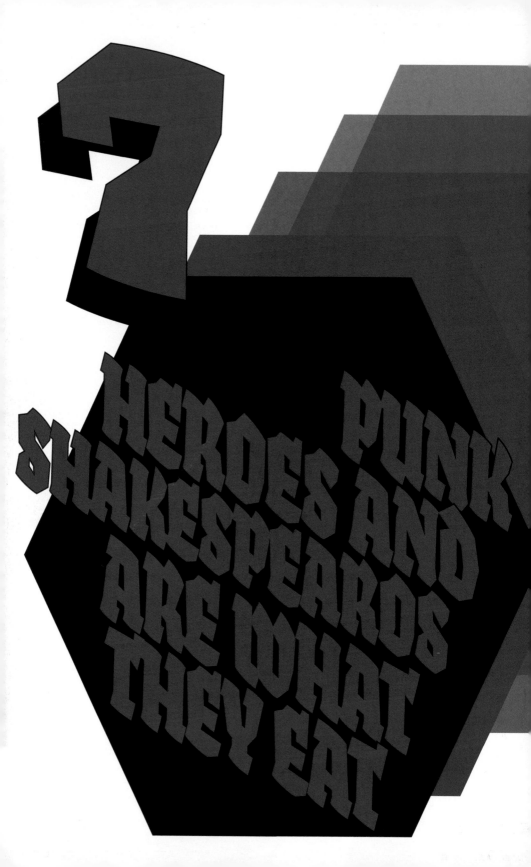

PUNK HEROES AND SHAKESPEARDS ARE WHAT THEY EAT

Haven't you always imagined certain punk performers eating a certain thing? Yes? Good. Because so have I! They may like this or that, but there are particular things I have always wanted to stuff in their mouths. Or maybe something comes out of their mouth on a regular basis that could easily be interpreted into a dish. Or maybe you actually want to have them over (tie them to a chair) and feed them something they actually "love." Well now you can!

Sky's the limit for the imagination generation.

PUNK HEROES AND SHAKESPEAROS ARE WHAT THEY EAT

by Zack Carlson

We all know that punk demigods roam the earth, setting fire to homes and murdering police. To get those jobs done, they require fuel.

So it's only natural to visualize your rock idols wolfing down the sustenance that matches their particular personal style. For example, I picture Plastic Bertrand munching on a plate of day-glo pink pasta, or Sickie Wifebeater from The Mentors sucking on a maggot-ridden apple core he pulled out of a wino's corpse.

Of course, there are even more sumptuous items on the menu. While the Ramones didn't dine in the swankiest New York restaurants, the boys supposedly had a gourmet-caliber appreciation of pizza. And there's no question that heavy hitters like Poison Idea were born with an insatiable hunger for the finer things.

In this chapter, Joshua examines the caloric constructs that enlivened the punk palate, and—in some cases—could have been responsible for the very creation of punk legends. I mean, honestly... there'd be no Big Boys without a Biscuit!

Great! Here's a bunch of songs from fairly recent and newer bands of the last couple years!

1 - SURVIVAL KNIFE "NAME THAT TUNE"

2 - STAB CITY "COLISEUM" (Pizza. What's not to like about pizza?)

3 - HUMAN BEAST "BALUSTER"

4 - FIELDED "THE KEY" (Yes, I know I have techno and ambient stuff on here. This list is stuff I might actually listen to or go to. Come to think of it, I have seen all of these bands!)

5 - CURSE "DOG CATCHER" (Curse from Baltimore. I love this band!)

6 - BRIDGE "LET ME GO"

7 - SEWN LEATHER "BAD MAN REDUXXX" (He used to live in the nook under the stairs.)

8 - SWAHILI "VESTAL"

9 - MOM "STUFFED ANIMALS" (Hide in the back when she plays.)

10 - MOMENT TRIGGER "EYES RUN DRY"

11 - STRIPPER PUSSY "COP KISSER"

12 - HYSTERICS "DEFORMATIVE YEARS" (Best thing Olympia has done in a while.)

13 - DEADPRESSURE "PANTSCRAPPER"

14 - THOU "THEIR HOOVES CARVE CRATERS IN THE EARTH"

15 - ATRIARCH "ALTARS"

16 - COPS "ANGELA"

17 - CRUDE STUDS (ANYTHING)

18 - NATO COLES & THE BLUE DIAMOND BAND "I-94"

19 - GULL "FAST ENOUGH" (I think sometimes he also does the dishes when he plays.)

20 - JOHNNY UNICORN "SADNESS" AND "COMPANIONSHIP" (It really is epic. Like, AN epic.)

BIG STUFFED BISCUIT AND MILKSHAKE FOR RANDY "BISCUIT" TURNER

What do I envision Randy "Biscuit" Turner of Austin, TX's Big Boys eating? Why, a biscuit of course! But his story was not as simple or boring as just a plain old biscuit. So I've stuffed it! Plus, he was a big, sexy boy so I've included a big, sexy milkshake. In my mind, he is eating this somewhere in heaven right now!

"PUNK ROCK IS LIKE CORN: EVERY YEAR THERE IS A NEW CROP." EBB SHRED, THRASHER MAGAZINE, CA. 1983

-BISCUIT-
2 C. FLOUR
1/3 C. RICE FLOUR
1/3 C. TO 1/2 C. SHORTENING OR OIL
1 TSP. BAKING POWDER
1 TSP. CREAM OF TARTAR
SALT AND BLACK PEPPER TO TASTE *(prob 1/2 to 1 tsp. of salt)*
1 C. SOY MILK OR OTHER EQUIVALENT
A LITTLE SUGAR *is nice but of course not necessary*

-STUFFING-
1/2 C. MUSHROOMS
1/2 C. CHOPPED CABBAGE
1/3 C. ROASTED VEGGIE SAUCE *(ajvar, achar, or sofreto)*
1/4 C. CHOPPED ONIONS
2 MINCED GARLIC CLOVES
A FEW TSP. MINCED FRESH HERBS
SPICES TO TASTE—CHILI, CUMIN, CORIANDER, ETC.
SALT AND PEPPER
A LITTLE OIL TO FRY

-MILKSHAKE-
2 BANANAS
1/2 C. STRAWBERRIES
1/4 C. MELTED CHOCOLATE
1/2 C. COCONUT CREAM
1/2 C. COCONUT OR CASHEW MILK *(more as needed)*
1 TSP. LEMON OR LIME JUICE
6 PITTED DATES
SUGAR OR AGAVE TO TASTE
SALT AND VANILLA TO TASTE

Garnishes: halved strawberries, banana slices, toasted coconut, and shaved chocolate

Mix dry ingredients for the biscuit together. Gradually mix in the oil and liquid. Season to taste. Knead for about two minutes and set aside. Sauté the filling in oil except for the ajvar, for six minutes. Mix the ajvar in and turn off heat, allow to cool. Roll out the dough into a big oval on a floured board, until about 1" thick. Stuff with the filling, fold, seal, and shape into a big round biscuit. Place on a lightly greased baking pan and brush with oil. Bake at 450 for around 20 minutes, it might take a bit less or more time, until the biscuit is browned. Blend all of the milkshake ingredients together except garnishes. Chill.

Garnish and serve on the side with the delicious biscuit, and listen to the Big Boys.

VEGAN ESCARGOT AND BLACK QUINOA CAVIAR FOR JELLO BIAFRA

Haha, poor Jello they all think he's some super rich guy in a mansion somewhere. Well, he certainly deserves some of the finer things in life, I'll say that. At some point you do just kinda earn respect, n'est-ce pas? This will definitely be less disgusting than real snails.

1 C. STRAW MUSHROOMS
1/2 C. BLACK QUINOA COOKED IN OLIVE JUICE *(yeah, how about that!!)*
1 TSP. CURRANT JELLY
2 TSP. SEAWEED FLAKE
1 TSP. GROUND BLACK SESAME
1 1/2 TSP. TOASTED RICE POWDER
2 PRESSED GARLIC CLOVES
2 TSP. OLIVE OIL/MARGARINE
LEMON
1/4 C. CHOPPED PARSLEY
2 MINCED SCALLIONS
SEA SALT TO TASTE

Straw mushrooms as is, are pretty creepy. Well, sauté them with garlic in oil for two minutes, then add a little salt and pepper, 1/2 tsp. rice powder, scallions, and parsley and remove from heat. Serve with lemon wedges.

Mix quinoa with currant jelly, sea salt, 1 tsp. rice powder, black sesame, and seaweed flake while still warm. Adjust seasonings and chill. A little oil may be added. Serve with little rye toasts, dill, and vegan cream cheese *(If you're into that stuff!)*.

PEACH MELBA AND KIR ROYALE
FOR DAVID JOHANSEN FROM THE NEW YORK DOLLS

-PEACH MELBA-
**2 C. COCONUT CREAM
1/3 C. SUGAR
PINCH OF SALT
INSIDES OF A VANILLA BEAN**

Purée this and freeze, stirring occasionally.

**2 PEACHES
1/4 C. SLIVERED ALMONDS
1 C. RASPBERRIES
1 TSP. LEMON JUICE
3/4 C. SUGAR
1 TSP. VANILLA
1/4 C. PEACH JUICE**

Halve and pit the peaches. Poach them in a cup of water with 1/2 C. sugar until soft. Meanwhile, toast the almond slivers in a dry pan and set aside. Mix the raspberries, lemon juice, 1/4 C. sugar, and peach juice, and simmer for five minutes. Add vanilla. Serve by placing two scoops of ice cream, then the warm peach, then several tsp. of raspberry sauce and top with slivered almonds. Delightful!

KIR ROYALE:
**4 PARTS CHAMPAGNE/SPARKLING WINE
1 PART CREME DE CASSIS
RASPBERRIES
CURRANTS**

Add champagne in a flute to the liqueur. Add a few berries and serve. Feel sassy.

This recipe suits that elegant lady, David Johanssen. I'll bet his arrival could inspire hotel chefs to create special desserts to soothe his vocal chords, much like what happened to Ms. Melba (And also melba toast happened to her, but maybe we'll get to that in the next book).

REFRIED BEANS PIZZA FOR JOEY RAMONE

Sitting there in Queens in Heaven, eating refried beans. Remember that one scene in Rock and Roll High School?! The poor guy deserves a pizza!

1/4 C. CHOPPED CILANTRO
1/2 C. CHOPPED OLIVES
1 C. SALSA
1 PIZZA CRUST *(use the pizza crust from the troubleshooting chapter)*
2 C. PINTO BEANS
1 1/2 TSP. CHILI POWDER
3 TSP. SHORTENING
1/4 TSP. LIQUID SMOKE
3 GARLIC CLOVES, PRESSED
1 ONION, MINCED OR GROUND
SALT AND PEPPER TO TASTE
A LITTLE OLIVE OIL
LIME JUICE
HOT SAUCE

Soak beans in 6 C. of water overnight. Change the water and simmer the beans for 1 1/2 hours, until soft. When the beans are done, drain them, reserving 1 C. of the bean liquid. Sauté onion, garlic, salt, and pepper in a few tbsp. olive oil in a large skillet for several minutes. Add beans and cook for several minutes more. Mash the beans, onions, etc. with reserved bean liquid, chili powder, black pepper, liquid smoke, shortening, salt to taste and some olive oil. Bring the skillet back to medium heat and fry until it begins to develop a bit of a crust in places. This will take around ten minutes. Add more bean liquid or shortening if you need to. Add lime juice, hot sauce, and more salt to taste. Roll out pizza crust and place on pizza pan. Slather with salsa and refried beans, decorate with olives and cilantro, and bake at 425 for 20-25 minutes. Feel free to add some cheesy crap.

LAVENDER TEA CAKES WITH EARL GREY FOR JOHN LYDON

Our lady Rotten will sit atop his tower of money, and sneer at you in his pajamas, while sipping tea with his pinkie out. and enjoying delicious crumpets. Well, tea cakes at least. Lavender represents the effete tastes of the British Empirrrrrrrrre.

**3 C. FLOUR
1 TSP. BAKING SODA
1 1/2 TSP. BAKING POWDER
1 C. LAVENDER SUGAR
3/4 C. SOY MILK OR OTHER YUMMY MILK
1/2 C. MARGARINE OR COCONUT OIL
1 TEASPOON VANILLA
2 TSP. LAVENDER FLOWERS
A FEW PINCHES SALT** *(to taste)*
2 TSP. LEMON JUICE

Mix flour, baking soda, baking powder, lavender flowers, sugar, and salt. Cut in margarine until mixture resembles crumbs. Add the wet ingredients and mix. Roll out gently on floured board to 1/2" thickness and cut into circles or squares. Bake on lightly greased (or parchmented) cookie sheets at 350 for 15-20 until golden. Serve with earl grey tea and an extended pinky. Or get some black tea, and mix with dried bergamot flowers and extract of bergamot orange rind, and make tea from that. But you're a punk, you're not gonna do that!

EXPLODING VOLCANO HOT DOG SURPRISE
FOR WENDY O. WILLIAMS

She will blow up all hella shit. And cut your dick off!

Long live Wendyyyyyyyyyyyyyyy!

8 VEGAN HOT DOGS
4 VEGAN BUNS
2 C. OF CHILI *(any of the chilies in any of my books will do)*
1/2 C. SALSA *(ditto)*
1/2 C. SAUERKRAUT
1 C. SLICED ONIONS
OIL FOR SAUTÉ
1 SQUARE BITTERSWEET CHOCOLATE
2 MINCED SCALLIONS
1/2 C. VEGAN "SOUR CREAM"

-SPARKLERS-
EITHER A LITTLE TIN OR VOTIVE HOLDER
WITH DRY ICE (ADD WATER) OR A FOIL CONE
WITH BAKING SODA (ADD VINEGAR)

Some malt vinegar would also fit in with this recipe. I'd also add french fries, but we already did that for the anarchy burger. To tell you the truth, if you put this on top of the anarchy burger, then actually blow it up, it might be even better...

Toast the buns and grill the dawgs. Heat the chili, and fry the onions and sauerkraut. Make two holes somewhere in each bun. Arrange buns with the hot dogs sticking up out of them in a great pile with the chili, layering with sauerkraut, salsa, onions, and sour kreem. Sprinkle with scallions and grate some of that chocolate on there. Place the cone or votive down in the top of this mess somewehere. Stick the sparklers in the chili. Add the vinegar to the baking soda in the cone or the water to the dry ice *(whichever method)*. Light the sparklers. Stand back, and oh yeah never EVER d...oh forget it! I love the Plasmatics!

TOMATOES FOUR WAY FOR TOMATA DU PLENTY

the Screamers were pretty innovative and Tomata did a lot of cool art and such, so he gets an interesting send off here.

But anyone would love this!

- TOMATO BREAD-

1 C. WARM TOMATO JUICE
2 TSP. DRY ACTIVE YEAST
1 TSP. OLIVE OIL
1 TSP. SMOKED PAPRIKA
1 TSP. GARLIC POWDER
1 TSP. SUGAR
1 TSP. SALT
3 C. FLOUR
2 TSP. TOMATO PASTE
1/3 C. GROUND TOMATOES

Activate yeast with water and sugar. Add oil, paprika, garlic powder, and other tomato stuff. Add salt and then the flour, working into a nice ball of dough. Add more liquid if need be. It should remain a bit sticky, even after kneading. Knead for ten minutes, oil lightly and place covered in a bowl for an hour or two. Knead into oblong loaf shape on a floured board, and place on a lightly greased and floured or be-corned baking sheet or in a large loaf pan. Let it rise again, covered gently. If using the baking sheet, you might have to push the sides in a little before baking. You can also score the dough gently diagonally, but it's not necessary. Bake at 375 for 25-30 or until done and crusty. To serve you'll cut into slices and toast them on a baking sheet before topping with everything else.

-FRIED TOMATOES-

This is easy, slice some tomatoes *(yes, green is fine)*, drain them, dust with a little salt and pepper, coat them in seasoned cornmeal and fry in light oil, turning once, until browned on both sides. Set aside.

-TOMATO SALAD-
Toss together

1 DICED TOMATO
1/4 C. CHOPPED OLIVES
1 TSP. CAPERS
1 TSP. OLIVE OIL
1 TSP. BALSAMIC VINEGAR
2 TSP. MINCED BASIL
1 TSP. MINCED ITALIAN PARSLEY
1/2 C. CHOPPED ARUGULA
CHILI FLAKES TO TASTE

-TOMATO SAUCE-
Blend

1/4 C. SUNDRIED TOMATOES
1 TSP. OLIVE OIL
1 TSP. LEMON JUICE
SALT AND PEPPER AND CHILI POWDER TO
TASTE
1 TSP. RED WINE
1 PEELED GARLIC CLOVE
2 TSP. PIMIENTOS

One goes on top of the other and voila! Where have I heard that before?

RIP HER TO SHREDS FOR DEBBIE HARRY

Debbie Harry looks good. She must eat her ass a big ol' salad every day. She's also sophisticated. And sassy. So is this. A little attitude and a lot going on...

1 C. DAIKON, JULIENNE
1 C. SNOW PEAS, CUT INTO THIN STRIPS
1/2 C. PLUMS, CUT INTO STRIPS
1 C. ASIAN PEAR, CUT INTO MATCHSTICKS
4 OZ. RICE NOODLES (DRY WEIGHT), COOKED
AND DRAINED
1/2 C. GRATED OR RIBBONED CARROT
2 TSP. GRATED GALANGAL/GINGER (OR BOTH)
1 TSP. MINCED LEMONGRASS
1 EACH RED, ORANGE AND GREEN BELL
PEPPERS, CHIFFONADE
1/2 C. THAI BASIL, CUT INTO THIN STRIPS
1/2 C. MINT CUT INTO THIN STRIPS
1 TSP. TOASTED RICE POWDER
2 TBSP. SEASONED RICE VINEGAR
2 TSP. SESAME OIL
1/4 C. CHOPPED GARLIC CHIVES
1/4 C. ROASTED SOY NUTS OR WASABI PEAS
A FEW TSP. SWEET/SPICY CHILI GARLIC SAUCE

Toss together and season to taste. Alternately, you can reserve a little of everything shredded and decorate the top with it.

TIDY HENRY
FOR HENRY ROLLINS

With all of that shouting, and yelling, and man poetry, I would expect Rollins to eat a manwich. Yet he is sensitive, and these days seems more like a sweater wearing dad. And some works of fan-fiction has him in "less traditional" mantasy roles, so I thought I would give this a kinder, gentler touch. Additionally it could be in the re-imagined vegan recipes chapter under "Sloppy Joe." It could be called "Tidy Joe" or maybe "Tidy Henry." And when you get older, you need healthier things to imbibe and munch on. And flax crackers so he can keep his movements regular.

SEVERAL LARGE ROMAINE LEAVES
1 C. COOKED BULGHUR OR QUINOA
1/2 C. COOKED PIGEON PEAS OR YELLOW SPLIT PEAS
1 C. CHOPPED FRESH TOMATOES
1/2 C. CHOPPED ROASTED PEPPERS
1/2 C. DELICIOUS BROTH
2-3 TBSP. SUNFLOWER OIL
1/2 C. CHOPPED RED ONIONS
2 PEELED GARLIC CLOVES
A FEW TBSP. MINCED CILANTRO
2 MINCED SCALLIONS
THINLY SLICED ZUCCHINI OR CUCUMBER
1 1/2 TSP. SMOKED PAPRIKA
1 TSP. GROUND CORIANDER
1/2 TSP. CINNAMON
1-2 TSP. MINCED DRIED CHILIES
SALT, PEPPER AND TAMARI TO TASTE
2-3 TBSP. MINCED PRESERVED LEMON
1 TBSP. CAPERS
1 TSP. BALSAMIC VINEGAR
1 TSP. CIDER VINEGAR OR MALT VINEGAR

optional: ethiopian spices are nice in this dish

-FLAX CRACKER-
1/2 C. FLAX SEEDS
1/4 C. SUNFLOWER SEEDS
1 TBSP. OIL
SALT, PEPPER AND GARLIC TO TASTE
1/2 C. BROTH
1/2 C. CHOPPED KALE OR COLLARD GREENS

For the **CRACKER**, purée ingredients until smooth, adjust seasonings. Pour and spread thin on a 9x13 lightly greased or parchment/nonstick covered baking pan *(must have sides of course!)*

Slow bake at 300 for about an hour, checking every now and again. The liquid should all bake off and it will have a cracker-like consistency. It might take a while longer, essentially you are dehydrating but at a higher temperature.

If you have a dehydrator, this would be a 6 hour/overnight job in trays. A little before they are done, score them so that they are easier to break apart. Take the zucchini/cucumber and sprinkle with salt, cider or malt vinegar and oil and bake this as well while the crackers are baking but for about 20 minutes less time.

Marinate red onion in balsamic vinegar with a pinch of salt while this is going on. For the rest, purée tomatoes, roasted bell pepper, broth, chili, spices, and oil. Cook over medium heat, stirring for 15 minutes, then add bulghur, peas, salt/pepper/tamari *(and anything else you feel like adding)* and cook for 10 minutes more.

Adjust seasonings to taste. Add more liquid if need be.

To serve, take a lettuce leaf and on one end place a cracker piece, followed by a scoop of "Tidy Henry," then sprinkle with cilantro, scallion and capers, top with another piece of cracker and fold lettuce leaf over the top to eat.

Serve with sweet chili sauce. Why? Cause I'm a lie-yar!

8.

NOT YOUR GRANDPA'S HARDCORE VEGAN SLOP

A punk plate of brown and brown and brown. With a side of greens. The old worn out pages of your favorite cookzine sticking haphazardly out of your back pocket, exploding with wild dreams of nutritional yeast gravy and cumin soaked lentils. That favorite casserole of rice puffkin that one dirtbag brought to the potluck that one time. Let's relive the memories of the punk recipes of the past. Retold! By someone with taste, that gives a shit!

Not Your Grandpa's Hardcore Vegan Slop

by Joe Biel

They're still lingering all over the nooks and crannies of the United States, from major urban areas to small town main streets. The smells wafting off of them are often enough to make you flinch or retreat in fear, even if you don't notice how unclean they are. You may never choose to engage but you're likely familiar with them. You've seen them around and had at least some curiosity. You hear the darndest things as you pedal by.

Yes, old school vegan restaurants might be even older than punk rock. They are definitely older than punk rockers, and often have a grisly secret or two lingering in their pasts, from sex cults to crazed owners with wild tempers to weird religions to tax embezzlement. From the pent-up aggro-hippies that tend to own them to the utter lack of managerial oversight going on inside of them, you've probably been steering clear for years.

But we all have our weaknesses. And there is that one menu item at each one that, on the off chance that the cook follows the recipe correctly and has fresh ingredients, tastes totally amazing and unlike any other flavenoids you've ever experienced.

Because of this difficult interactive slam dance, The Joshua Ploeg Punk Rock Franchise offers you Vegan Classics Re-imagined. Maybe you weren't lucky enough to grow up near one of these eyesore holdovers of the 1970s, but you've likely been "treated" to a plate of plain tofu and vegetables in some sort of "broth." At least I was.

The restaurant Tommy's in Cleveland still serves a savory "pie" *(mysteriously titled "MR-4")* made out of peanut butter, banana, various vegetables, and cinnamon. It's baked, tastes like absolutely nothing I've eaten before or since, and definitely left me with a flawed impression of what vegans eat.

So without further ado, let us fix the acid-damaged creations of post-hippie cuisine!

Like a fabulous recipe of yore redid-ID, here are some cover songs...*(we'll go back and forth from pretty straight to pitchfork-and-torches worthy)*

1 - MELVINS "VENUS IN FURS"
2 - PANSY DIVISION WITH CALVIN JOHNSON "JACKSON"
3 - RAMONES "PALISADES PARK"
4 - JAWBREAKER "INTO YOU LIKE A TRAIN"
5 - FRIGHTWIG "PUBLIC BATHS"
6 - THE ACCUSED "HIGHWAY STAR"
7 - VOIVOD "ASTRONOMY DOMINE"
8 - BLACK FAG "GIMME GIMME GIMME"
9 - COCKWIND "URBAN GUERILLA"
10 - 3 TEENS KILL 4 "TELL ME SOMETHING GOOD"
11 - DEAD KENNEDYS "BACK IN THE USSR"
12 - THE CONVOCATION OF "GET DOWN MAKE LOVE"
13 - PRIMAL SCREAM "SLIP INSIDE THIS HOUSE"
14 - SONIC YOUTH "BURNING FARM"
15 - GET HUSTLE "ANOTHER ONE BITES THE DUST"
16 - BUTTHOLE SURFERS "EARTHQUAKE"
17 - MUDHONEY "HATE THE POLICE"
18 - CHEMICAL PEOPLE "DEVIL HOUSE"
19 - RESIDENTS "IT'S A MAN'S WORLD"
20 - LAIBACH "I ME MINE"
21 - DOS MUJERES UN CAMINO "SUSPECT DEVICE"
22 - NINE INCH NAILS "GET DOWN MAKE LOVE"

THE OL' VEGGIE FRIED CHICKN, MASHED POTATOES, GRAVY AND GREENS RE-ENVISIONED

-CHICKN FRIED TOFU-

1 BLOCK TOFU, CUT INTO 1/2" THICK LITTLE SQUARES
1/2 C. TAMARI (OR OTHER MARINADE)
SAGE AND OTHER HERBS
1/2 TSP. CORIANDER
CURRY POWDER (TURMERIC HEAVY)
SALT AND PEPPER
1 C. FLOUR
1/2 C. BEER OR SODA

-MASHED POTATOES-

2 C. COOKED POTATOES
1/2 C. OF THE POTATO WATER
SEVERAL TBSP. OLIVE OIL
SOME MINCED CHIVES AND ITALIAN PARSLEY
3 OR 4 MINCED GARLIC CLOVES

-GRAVY-

1 C. CHOPPED MUSHROOMS
A FEW TBSP. FLOUR
CUMIN, SMOKED SALT, HERBS, SALT AND PEPPER TO TASTE
1/2 C. CHOPPED ONION
2 MINCED GARLIC CLOVES
1 C. OR MORE MUSHROOM OR VEGGIE BROTH
1 SWEET POTATO

-GREENS-

1 HEAD CHOPPED GREENS
1/2 C. SLICED ONION
A LITTLE BALSAMIC
SALT AND PEPPER
OIL TO SAUTÉ

-GARNISH-
RED CHILIES OR SEASONED BELL PEPPER

Roast the sweet potato. Poke a bunch of holes in it with a fork (wash it first) and bake at 375 minutes, turning here and there for about 45 to an hour. Then mash it.

Marinate the **TOFU** with tamari, sage and coriander, turning/coating repeatedly for while. Season with a bit of curry, salt and pepper. Mix the flour, beer and more salt and pepper and curry together *(the dreaded nutritional yeast may also be added)*. Coat the tofu in this business thoroughly. Fry in some oil, turning, until browned and crispy.

Mash the **POTATOES** with the rest of their friends to taste. Toast the flour in a saucepan for about a minute. Whisk in oil, then the liquid (methodically).

Separately sauté the mushrooms, onion, garlic, and herbs for several minutes, then add them to the **GRAVY**. Season to taste, add more liquid as needed.

Sauté the **GREENS** and onion in oil. After five minutes, add a bit of balsamic, salt and pepper, and a little water. Cover and cook for 10-15 minutes, then remove the lid and cook until done to your liking.

For composition, use a wine or cocktail glass. Place some potatoes in the bottom, followed by sweet potatoes, thin layer of greens, a little gravy in there perhaps, then a little more potatoes, sweet potatoes, chickn and gravy, with a fountain of greens on top. Arrange pepper spikes attractively around the glass. Of course, for larger portions use a humongous wine glass. And if you make the layers thinner you can have more layers for ambitious striping

ZUCCHINI BREAD

A much daintier version of a fine basic item that a lot of people screw up. I like zucchini bread. But there was a time when it ruled the land like a great zucchinasaurus, stomping all over the place creating havoc. Basically, it has always been the sort of vegetable which is cheap/free and easy to come by, and which any dipshit can successfully grow. And grow way, way too large without harvesting. Until it is so biiiig that only zucchini bread can be made from it. Anyway, do not use a huge zucchini for this, use little tasty ones.

**1 C. GRATED ZUCCHINI
1/4 C. GRATED CARROT
1/4 C. AGAVE OR MAPLE SYRUP
1/2 TSP. GRATED GINGER
1 1/2 TSP. MIXED MINCED LEMON AND ORANGE PEEL
1/2 C. GOLDEN RAISINS
SEA SALT TO TASTE
SCRAPINGS OF 1 VANILLA BEAN
1/2 TSP. EACH GROUND CINNAMON, ALLSPICE, CLOVE, GINGER
1/4 C. GRATED COCONUT
1/2 C. CHOPPED PECANS AND HAZELNUTS
1 MASHED BANANA
2 TSP. LEMON JUICE
2 TSP. OIL
12 THIN SLICES OF ZUCCHINI, BLANCH THEM IN SUGAR WATER AND DRAIN, THEN SPRINKLE WITH A LITTLE CINNAMON SUGAR** *(or just make them verrry thin to keep with the raw theme)*

Mix together all but the zucchini slices, reserving a couple of Tbsp. of nuts and raisins and a little lemon peel *(you could do ribbons for garnish)*. Adjust seasonings to taste. Roll up in the zucchini slices. Garnish these with remaining nuts, raisins and lemon peel. Pretty fun variation there!

MATE LATTE

All punks love coffee, but suppose you've outgrown it or are too good for that. Instead, they drink mate like a hippy. Well, that won't do either. So let's compromise and make something that nobody will like. Just kidding. It's great.

1 C. DRY MATE
1 C. COCONUT MILK
(OPTIONAL: 1 OR 2 TSP. SOY LECITHIN)
WATER

Toast mate in dry pan until it's browning and smells interesting/toasty. But don't burn it! Grind it in batches for 15 seconds in a coffee grinder for a relatively fine grind. Use as you would coffee grounds in espresso maker or mocha pot, except: you need to wet the "grounds" before running hot water through in order to avoid too bitter of a taste, *m'kay!* Take two shots of this "matte espresso" and pour into a mug. Take 1/4 C. coconut milk per beverage and mix in a little lecithin (like half a teaspoon) and froth with your steaming wand, or heat in a saucepan over medium/high whisking the shit out of it until it is a bit frothy. Spoon onto your espresso. That's what lecithin does. Whisking lecithin and liquid viciously is also a way to make culinary foam, if that's still a thing. Actually, if it's super passe, even better! Then it fits right in with our whole punk rock theme so well!

JICAMA "POTATO" SALAD

Well shoot me, it's not just old punk cookbooks with boring recipes for potato salad. Really, the variations on this can be mind blowing but people like what they like. Because it's "traditional," the definition of which has been stretched to the point of pointlessness. Do what you want, but stop being fucking boring! If you hate crunchiness this recipe will be your worst enemy due to jicama's unwavering crunch.

**3 C. DICED JICAMA
1 CUCUMBER (OR ZUCCHINI), CUT INTO STRIPS
1 C. COOKED GARBANZO BEANS
1/2 C. MINCED RED BELL PEPPER
1/4 C. MINCED RED ONION
GREEN BELL PEPPER
1 TSP. CHILI FLAKES OR 1 TBSP CHILI SAUCE** *(less or more to taste)*
**1/4 C. LIME JUICE
3-4 TBSP. OLIVE OIL
SALT AND PEPPER TO TASTE
1 BULB OF ROASTED GARLIC, PEELED
A HANDFUL OF CHOPPED CILANTRO
1/2 C. DELICIOUS PEAS
2 DICED CARROTS
1/2 C. CIDER VINEGAR
1 TSP. ONION POWDER**

Heat vinegar with onion powder and some salt to a simmer. Add cucumber and turn off heat. Allow to sit for 15 to an hour.

Place garbanzo beans in a baking dish and baste with oil, sprinkle with salt and pepper and any spices you may enjoy and roast at 425 for 15-20 minutes, turning once until crunchy on the outside. These are a great addition to just about anything!

Blend roasted garlic, olive oil, salt and lime juice. Adjust seasonings to taste. You could also add sunflower seeds, tahini, or other substances to the mix when blending. A teaspoon or two of cider vinegar won't kill it either. This is your dressing, so you want it to be how you want it!

Toss the other ingredients together with a little salt and pepper *(keeping in mind how salty the dressing is)*. Drain and chop the cucumber and add that in, followed by the dressing. Re-season to taste. Serve chilled or as is.

LENTIL LOAF

This is the true potluck nightmare! This is what people think of when they imagine vegan-punk food *(especially free food)*. That and bagels. Well, certainly something can be done with lentils. Something else! I've included a vaguely fishy topping because, well, I can! And it's good. Also, we're gonna help you get rid of that jar of capers. If you don't like 'em, use olives or something. Do I have to s-p-e-l-l everything one can do out to people? Having been around long enough, I can truly say...yes. Yes, I do have to spell it out. Anyway, feel free to replace anything in this book with anything else.

-CRACKER-
2 C. LENTIL FLOUR
1/4 C. GROUND FLAX SEEDS
1/4 C. TAPIOCA FLOUR
1/3 C. COCONUT OIL OR PALM OIL (OR MARGARINE)
1/2 C. WATER (MORE AS NEEDED)
1/4 C. SESAME SEEDS
2 TBSP. GARLIC OR ONION FLAKES
2 TBSP. ONION POWDER
1/2 TSP. SALT
2 TSP. GARLIC POWDER
1 TSP. CURRY POWDER
1 TSP. CRUSHED CUMIN SEEDS

Mix the flours and flax seeds together. Add in the oil to crumb. Add the other ingredients and mix well, using enough water to make a workable dough. Roll out as thinly as you like between two sheets of parchment. Carefully remove the top parchment and then cut your desired cracker shapes. Bake at 350 on a baking sheet *(you shouldn't have to oil the sheet)* for several minutes, until crispy. Keep an eye on them.

2 TBSP. ROASTED SEAWEED
1 C. COOKED GARBANZO BEANS
1/4 C. CHOPPED ONION
2 TBSP. OLIVE OIL
1 TBSP. LEMON JUICE
2 PEELED GARLIC CLOVES
1 TBSP. FRESH DILL
1 TBSP. PREPARED MUSTARD
1/4 C. CHOPPED TOMATO
SALT AND PEPPER TO TASTE

Blend this in a food processor,
serve with crackers and relish.

-RELISH-
1 TBSP. CAPERS
1 TBSP. MINCED ITALIAN PARSLEY
2 TBSP. BALSAMIC VINEGAR
2 MINCED SCALLIONS
SALT TO TASTE TO TASTE
CHILI FLAKES
1 OR 2 TSP. OLIVE OIL

Toss this and serve atop crackers and spread.

This is an amusing way to tell people you made "lentil surprise!"

MAC N CHEEZ WITH TVP CHILI & ACOUTREMENTS

Here we combine two fairly easy, often terrible dishes into one new improved thing you could serve to a person without proving that you secretly hate them.

Enjoy!

1 C. DRY LENTILS
1 C. DRY TVP
4 C. FAVORITE VEGGIE BROTH *(more as needed)*
1 C. DICED EGGPLANT
2 C. CRUSHED TOMATOES
2 TBSP. TAMARIND LIQUID
1 C. CHOPPED MUSHROOMS
3 MINCED GARLIC CLOVES
1 OR 2 MINCED CHILIES
1 C. CHOPPED ONION
A TSP. OF CUMIN
A TSP. OF CHILI POWDER
1/4 C. TOMATO PASTE
SOME BLACK PEPPER
1/2 TSP. CINNAMON
1/2 TSP. GROUND CORIANDER
1/4 C. ESPRESSO
1/4 C. PURÉED SUNDRIED TOMATOES
1 TSP. DRIED OREGANO
1 TBSP. MINCED CILANTRO
SALT AND TAMARI TO TASTE
CHILI SAUCE TO TASTE
1/2 C. CHOPPED BELL PEPPER

Start by cooking the lentils in veggie broth. After ten minutes add soy chunks, spices, tomato products and tamari to taste. Add more water to cover if need be, then add everything else and cook for 30 minutes, stirring occasionally and covering for half the time. Adjust seasonings to taste all the while. If your lentils take longer than this to cook *(some varieties do)*, cook them by themselves longer before adding the rest of the stuff.

NUTRITIONAL YEAST MAC N CHEEZ

2 C. COOKED PASTA
1/4 C. SAUERKRAUT,
1/3 C. CASHEWS,
2 TBSP. MISO,
1 TBSP. PREPARED MUSTARD,
SALT AND WHITE PEPPER TO TASTE,
1/4 C. DICED ONION,
2 TBSP. LEMON JUICE *(or more)*
A SPLASH OF WHITE BALSAMIC OR RED WINE VINEGAR,
1/2 TO 1 C. MUSHROOM BROTH *(more or less depending on thickness you want)*
1/4 C. TAHINI
2 OR 3 GARLIC CLOVES,
2 TBSP. TAPIOCA OR POTATO STARCH
2-3 TBSP. NUTRITIONAL YEAST.

Blend everything together but the pasta and season to taste.

Cook over low heat, stirring until it thickens up a bit. Stir in pasta. Finish seasoning to taste.

Place the mac in a bowl, top with a few dollops of chili and then...

Top further with:
LEEKS, CAPERS, PICKLED PEPPERCORNS HEIRLOOM TOMATOES WITH POM VINAIGRETTE

TOFU SCRAMBLE

Every vegan cookzine ever has a recipe for this in it. It's a vegan brunch/ breakfast staple! We will jazz up the tofu scramble by making it into a tasty, fancy version of something a lot of people do badly: chilaquiles!

1 1/2 C. CHOPPED HUITLACOCHE *(instantly this makes the dish cost several times as much. But why stop there—use fresh porcini or morels!)* **OR USE SHIITAKE OR CRIMINI**
8-12 CORN TORTILLAS, CUT INTO STRIPS
(we're gonna make a big batch)
1 ONION, DICED
2 MINCED GARLIC CLOVES, 2 WHOLE CLOVES
CHIPOTLE SAUCE TO TASTE, PROBABLY ABOUT 1/2 C. TO A CUP, *depending on how saucy you like it, water down some paste with a bit of tomato sauce and some water or broth to make it less spicy*
1 OR 2 DICED BELL PEPPERS
1 TSP. MINCED JALAPENO
OIL TO DRIZZLE/COAT
SALT TO TASTE
1/2 C. CHOPPED CILANTRO
1 TSP. CUMIN
1 1/2 TSP. CHILI POWDER
A FEW DASHES LIME JUICE
2 C. TOFU OR CANNELINI BEANS
1/4 C. CIDER VINEGAR
1/4 C. RICE FLOUR
1 TSP. MINCED OREGANO
*- optional: **1 C. COOKED BLACK BEANS,** *throw those in there for the baking when the chipotle sauce is added*
PLUS:
1 LB. TOFU
1/2 C. DICED ONION
1 TBSP. CURRY POWDER
SALT, PEPPER AND TAMARI TO TASTE
2 MINCED GARLIC CLOVES
1 TSP. CHILI POWDER
1/2 C. DICED BELL PEPPER
OIL TO SAUTÉ

Coat a baking dish with some oil, place tortilla strips and onion in there and toss/coat with oil, some salt and a bit of the chili powder and cumin. Bake at 400 for 10 minutes, toss and bake another 10 min. *(or until a bit crispy, might happen sooner)*. Now, mix the chipotle sauce, peppers, minced garlic, lime juice, oregano, the rest of the cumin and chili powder, and some salt. Toss with the tortilla strips and 1 C. of the huitlacoche, and bake 10 more minutes at 375. Now, mix the tofu or cannelini, cider vinegar, a little oil or earth balance, whole garlic cloves, rice flour, 1/2 C huitlacoche, salt to taste, and maybe a bit more spice. Blend until smooth. Toss a little cilantro on top of the tortilla concoction, then pour the creamy mixture over the top. Add the rest of the cilantro, a pinch of pepper and chili powder, and bake a final 10-15 minutes. The end. The baking time comes out to 45 minutes, typical for a casserole. You can do this on the stovetop as well, or start it there and then finish by baking the sauce on top.

While it's baking, cook everything in the "Plus:" section in a skillet over medium/med-high heat, turning occasionally with a spatula until browned. Serve a scoop of the tofu on a plate with a square of chilaquiles on top. And garnish with salsa fresca and arugula. There. Isn't that better?!

BURRITO
WITH CUCUMBER SALSA

1 PKG. SOY SKIN *(the dry but flexible kind)*
1/2 C. SLICED SHIITAKE MUSHROOMS
1/2 C. SLICED ZUCCHINI
1/2 C. CHOPPED MIXED BELL PEPPER
1 MINCED CHILI *(Or less, ya wuss!)*
LIME JUICE TO TASTE
1/4 C. DICED TOMATOES
1/4 C. DICED ONIONS
2 OR 3 MINCED GARLIC CLOVES
2 MINCED SCALLIONS OR 1 CEBOLLA
OIL FOR SAUTÉ
1/2 C. SEASONED COOKED RICE *would be nice.*
CHILI POWDER, SALT, PEPPER, CUMIN
AND CORIANDER TO TASTE
2 OR 3 TBSP. MINCED CILANTRO

-CUCUMBER SALSA-
1 C. PERSIAN CUCUMBERS, SLICED INTO
HALF MOONS
1 TSP. CAPERS OR CHOPPED GREEN
OLIVES
1/2 TSP. CHILI FLAKES OR 1 MINCED
SEEDED CHILI
CHILI POWDER, SALT, AND PEPPER TO
TASTE
1/2 TBSP. OLIVE OIL
2 TBSP. LIME JUICE
1 TBSP. MINCED CILANTRO
2 TBSP. MINCED ONION
1 MINCED GARLIC CLOVE

Rather than the oversized Mission-style beast that all the starving cheapskates love, I'm gonna take a different angle on this old faithful. Why more people don't make 'em this way, I'll never know! Hmm, yes—let's do this as a soy-skin Chimichanga instead. Everyone knows how to make a burrito. This will be crispy and interesting, and also it can be done without the aid of wheat or corn.

Sauté the mushrooms, garlic, onion, zucchini, and peppers in a little oil. Add seasonings, turn off heat and add other ingredients, except the soy skin. Season to taste. Cut the skin into large pieces that will be able to easily wrap around a burrito-amount of filling. Place filling in the skin pieces and roll them up in a nice, tight, burrito-y fashion. Fry in oil, turning once, until browned/crispy on both sides. You can also turn on its side and brown the sides. Overall, it's not that difficult.

Toss the **CUCUMBER SALSA** and serve with "burrito."

"I FELT BAD LIKING WHEAT GERM WHEN I FINALLY TRIED IT BECAUSE I THOUGHT ANYTHING WORTHY OF JOEY RAMONE'S SCORN WAS WORTHY OF MINE."- JOSH BROWN (MAN ABOUT TOWN)

BAKED SQUASH

Nothing could be more boring, and it is often overly seasoned with one spice (cumin) or served with—blech—sugar! Here we make squash better by giving it the Imam Bayildi eggplant treatment. The middle eastern fare spruces it right up! As always. Really, what do you want when your band tours the Netherlands? Veal balls? Or falafel? I rest my case!

1 LARGE SQUASH, SPLIT AND SEEDED, AND SCORED
1/2 C. WINE
2 C. DICED EGGPLANT
2 TBSP. TAHINI
1/2 C. ROASTED SHELLED PISTACHIOS
1/4 C. OLIVE OIL
1 C. DICED ONION
3 MINCED GARLIC CLOVES
1 OR 2 TBSP. CHILI SAUCE
1 TBSP. LEMON JUICE
1/2 C. TOMATO SAUCE *(or ajvar, even better)*
3 OR 4 TBSP. SEASONED BREAD CRUMBS
1 TBSP. MINCED OREGANO
2 TBSP. MINCED BASIL
1 TSP. GROUND SUMAC
2 TBSP. MINCED ITALIAN PARSLEY
1/4 C. CHOPPED ARTICHOKE HEARTS
1/4 C. CHOPPED SUNDRIED TOMATOES
1 TSP. ASAFOETIDA
2 TSP. CURRY POWDER
1/2 TSP. CUMIN
1 TSP. CHILI POWDER

Place squash halves in a casserole with a little water and sprinkle with oil, salt and pepper. Roast at 400 for 40 minutes. Meanwhile sauté eggplant, onion, garlic in olive oil for several minutes. Add the rest, reserving some pistachios and herbs and remove from heat. Stuff squash halves with this mixture, seasoning to taste and bake for a further 20 minutes. Sprinkle with pistachios and herbs and serve. Nice with extra ajvar or tomato sauce on the side. Good with rice.

GLOSSARY

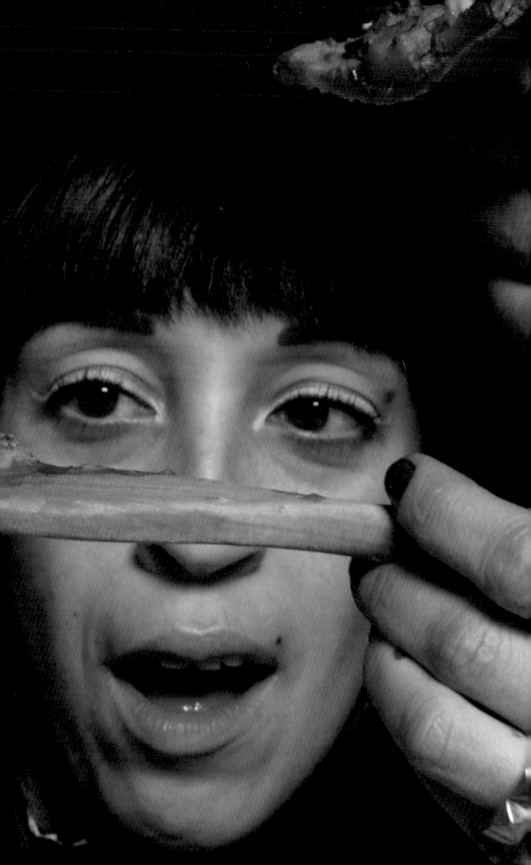

AJVAR/ACHAR
This is a tasty blend of roasted vegetables (usually eggplant, peppers, onion and garlic) with spices and sunflower or olive oil. Comes in a jar from a middle eastern or eastern european grocery, sometimes can be spicy, always delicious. *Sofreto/sofrito* is similar and probably familiar to ya. It's good stuff. Also, not too tough to make from scratch. Roasted pepper purée or a spiced tomato purée are fine substitutions.

BAKING POWDER V. BAKING SODA
Both are rising agents. Although they rise with some similarity (because yes indeed baking powder usually has baking soda in it), soda has a bit more of an after taste or can be slightly more bitter in the same quantity. Probably because it doesn't have the fillers that powder has. Soda will tend to go flat in a batter if not used quickly (once liquid is added). Baking powder usually contains cream of tartar and a starch (thus, check the label if you have corn allergies). Double acting will be active after some time, single needs to be used sooner. Normally, you can substitute them 1:1 with the addition of a little starch or cream of tartar(depends on the other ingredients). If used quickly, soda water can be used instead of baking soda and some of the liquid in recipes. Substitutions besides soda water: dry yeast activated in a little warm water, beer, or any other form of fermentation. Have fun!

BASIL & THAI BASIL
There are many types of basil available for us to investigate these days. Thai basil tends to have a slight licoricey flavor and the leaves are longer, narrower and darker and it has a bit more pungent smell. Substituting one for the other can be a poor surprise if you don't know what to expect. Lemon basil has a slightly more house-cleaner appeal to it (yes, don't I make it sound delish!). To this effect, it can be a fun substitute for the others for that fresh, Pledge-y taste! Basil flowers can be nice in things and taste a bit peppery. But basil that has totally gone to seed tastes like shit, so don't let your garden overgrow, honeychild!

BERGAMOT FLOWERS – Bergamot is a

yellowish colored orange. The flowers, oil, and peel of which feature in the flavor of earl grey tea. It has a peculiar taste. You're peculiar.

BULGHUR – Wheat groats. Substitutions: quinoa, buckwheat,

millet, rice, etc. You're groats.

COCONUT – There are many ways to enjoy coconut. Can I tell you

how great frozen is? Next best thing to fresh. Coconut cream is more fat/meat than regular coconut milk, and is usually much thicker or completely solid like "cream cheese." Replace it with very thick homemade nut or seed milks, which you can make from scratch by simply soaking your nuts and puréeing them with water (and salt and/or sweetener if you wish), controlling the conistency by the amount of water used. Soy or oat milk that is thick can be used as the cream as well (or whatever), and any milk can replace the coconut milk. Any dried, shredded fruit can replace coconut shreds/meat. Easy peasy.

Coconut water is supposed to be good for a hangover but I dunno. Whenever I'm hungover and try to drink it, I barf.

Your nuts are soaked.

CREAM OF TARTAR – This is chiefly used as a

stabilizer or in baking powder to activate the soda. It also improves the texture of biscuits. "Potassium bitartrate," it's a by-product of wine making. You can just leave it out when it's mentioned here if you don't have any.

CRUSHED TOMATOES - As canned or boxed

tomatoes go, this is usually one of the better types. Go for one without much (if anything) added. The texture is a little ambiguous, having still some substance to it, so not a purée but not as chunky as diced, which I find pretty appealing. Of course if you can't find it just use some other magnificent tomato product.

What if you can't eat tomatoes? Water down some ajvar (mentioned above) which usually does not have any tomatoes in it.

Of course, if you can't eat tomatoes OR eggplant then you're fucked, right?! No, then you can have pepper purée or roasted pepper purée. Now if you can't eat ANY of those three things, then you're fucked! Seriously though, use roasted squash or carrots puréed with broth to replace the tomatoes then. You can add a little lemon juice, vinegar or other acid to amp up that missing aspect, and add basil, sage, rosemary or some piney herb for that slightly piney taste tomatoes often have. Viola!

DAIKON - This long, dong-looking radish is great. Usually it's

white, but can be a little green. Excellent grated or made into a pickle. Can be a little harsh, but usually to me it is less spicy than a regular radish. Subsitutes can include regular radishes, kohlrabi, rainbow carrots, raw zucchini, fresh horseradish, burdock root, and other such things if you can't find them or don't like them. Peel it first.

One exciting thing you can do with daikon is make a strip or ribbon the entire length of the thing! Which can be a couple of feet long. For presentation and amazement purposes this can be astounding!

DATES - There are many types of dates, your common ones around

these parts be:

*Deglet Noor- translucent golden on the inside, brownish out, a little dryer than medjool and less sweet with a slightly caramel-y flavor.

*Medjool- these are the big, brown sweet ones that are most common here, fairly moist. You're moist.

*Barhi- these are more roundish, rich and fairly soft and okay even when not dried (they will be yellowish in color then)

*Zahidi- sweet and light brown, smaller than medjool and less common in the US

*Empress/Thoory- empress is a larger, softer thoory of American origin, regular thoory are reddish brown, a bit hard, wrinkled and taste sort of nutty

Substitute: figs, prunes, tamarind, or other dried fruits you like better!

DURIAN–

When ripe this spiky-ass fruit has a soft, creamy texture, luxurious taste, and smells like ass. An acquired taste to some, but mostly due to the smell. In the US you are most likely to find it in the freezer at an Asian grocery store. Although they are popping up everywhere nowadays. Replace with chermoya (ah, this is a harder fruit like a mealy apple with oddly placed diagonal seeds that can taste vaguely of cheese) or papaya (which when ripe can taste a bit... ripe!).

Vaguely tastes of cheese. Yeah. Durian based uncheese will make any uncheese plate all that much more special and uncheesy.

FENNEL–

Comes in many forms, the mild tasting green bulb, stalk and thin leaves are quite nice. Really, people often think they don't like it but the licorice taste is quite mild. The little dried seeds are stronger in taste and you will recall them from your days of eating sausage. Use in moderation, those seeds. When crushed or toasted the fragrance becomes even more pronounced. The bulb is good for salads, pilafs, slaws and gratins particularly. Star anise is not fennel, it is a woody pod that comes off an evergreen shrub and has a very strong taste. Just mentioning this because sometimes people refer to fennel as "anise." Nope.

FENUGREEK–

This is often in curry spice mixes and Indian or Middle Eastern food. One of those spices that some people do not really like. And this might be one (or ginger or turmeric or cumin or anise or fennel) that puts some people off from curry when they say "I can't quite put a finger on what I don't like about it." It can have a bit bitter taste, and is nice toasted and crushed. The leaves are to die for and have a fresh, slightly musky taste and smell. The dried leaves are great when combined with lime peel and sour dishes.

GALANGAL
– This fabulous rhizome is similar to ginger but uglier and with a woody stalk in the center. Another item that tastes vaguely of household cleaner, but in a good way! If you've ever had tom yam kha, you've had galangal. Substitute: ginger, lime leaf or myrtle leaf, lemongrass, fenugreek, star anise, orange peel, or any combinations thereof. Slightly bitter herbs (such as epazote or hoja santa) mixed with ginger would be convincing. None of these really taste the same but you will be in the ballpark of curiosity.

Roasting a few slices in a toaster oven and adding to broth will make your soup quite tasty. Actually roasting anything you're making broth out of first will do that. Especially spices!

HUITLACOCHE
– "Corn smut" or "corn mushroom" is quite beloved in Mexico. American farmers throw it out, but they may come around eventually. Some call it "Mexican truffle." Please! It's not really that strong, and, while somewhat pricey, it's not thaaaat expensive. Canned or jar is fine. Just take out all of the corn silk. Compared to other mushrooms, huitlacoche has a lot of lysine in it. Whatever the heck that is! Generally it is used in empanadas and quesadillas. Substitute: mushrooms. Or a mild seaweed. Or eggplant or tempeh.

LAVENDER
– Use culinary lavender! Don't die! Haha jk. Lavender flowers are pretty easy to find in a bulk tea or herb section dried, so you can use them, and make your own lavender tea or water via infusion or decoction. Or decapitation. Whatever. Substitute: other dried flowers, poppy seeds, rosewater, orange blossom water, fancy mint (like chocolate mint, or of course, LAVENDER mint).

MINT
Explore mint. Add it even when I don't tell you to. Spearmint, peppermint, chocolate mint, Moroccan, pineapple, lavender. They all taste pretty different from each other. Usually I am using spearmint in savory dishes, and peppermint in sweets, beverages, or with fruit. But not always! Mwahahaha!

Of course, feel free to experiment. Makes a good replacement for cilantro if you hate that! Replacements for mint include: sage, lemon basil, thai basil, cilantro (each for the other!), epazote, tarragon, and watercress.

Personally I find this shit refeshing in many places. It will also tend to add a "What's that?" flavor when people don't suspect it to be in there.

MUSHROOMS
Come on ya love 'em! some varieties I use...

*Black Fungus- Also called cloud ear or wood ear. Normally it is dried and imported when you find it here. You would soak it in warm water for 15-30 minutes and then drain and use however you were going to use it. Can be a pretty springy/rubbery/chewy texture and doesn't have a heck of a lot of taste. Fresh wood ear from the US will taste better and be a less combative texture.

*Blewit- These are great, if you have any mycologist/foraging pals to get them for you. They're not a common store bought mushroom. They are rich and delicious, and yes, a little blueish-purple. Some people have a bad reaction to these compared to most other mushrooms (especially if they are eaten raw), and they should not be stored for very long when fresh. Good for simple dishes and stews.

*Button vs. Crimini- Really not that much different, crimini are generally older. Meanwhile portabello are beasically gihugic ones. Crimini can have a slightly mustier taste (but that might be psychological).

*Enoki- This is a crazy long, thin, white mushroom usually in a little bundle. Very delicate, they don't withstand long cooking times. I like to put them in sushi and spring rolls. Taste is very mild, texture a bit like cooked noodles.

*Lobster- A parasitic hoopadoop infests mushrooms and makes them a delicious lobster. Yes they're edible. A vaguely "oceany" taste and full flavor. These pretty much rule. The texture is great, they are dense and not really slimy, and can even have a bit of spicy/peppery flavor to them. Dried they are quite enticing in soups, and reconstituted and added to pot pies and other dishes. You are more likely to find them in the dry form.

*Maiitake- this is one of those crazy tree-fungusy looking buggers that grow in a fan-like cluster. Also called "hen of the woods." They have a pretty deep, maybe a little woodsy, flavor.

*Morel- expensive, these have the distinctive long, porous cap. Thus it's sometimes called "sponge mushroom." They have something of a nutty flavor, and people that love them reeallly love them. Best used in a simple manner and they don't do with a lot of washing.

*Oyster- These are grey and look sort of like oysters/clams/ears. Also known as abalone. They cook quickly and the taste is good, fairly mild, and they soak up some flavor! King oyster is more of a sort of meaty stalk and those are pretty great too and less slimy.

*Porcini- this is another rich, slightly nutty one. I love these little buggers. Dried they can impart a strong taste to broth or stew. The fresh are going to be expensive as hell but worth it if you only do it every once in a while. I like to split them, cook quickly in a tasty light marinade and use them to make little sliders.

*Shiitake- these you'll know. Nice strong taste. A lot of people discard the stems but not me! That is a tasty, meaty mushroom part there. But if you don't like them, use them to make broth! To me this has one of the most substantial textures of any mushroom. I use them the most often.

*Straw- they are picked before fully mature. They have some flavor, but are still pretty mild, and both slimy and chewy when cooked. One of the most popular mushrooms in the world. Usually you would need to go to an Asian (like, east Asian) grocery to find them. The canned can be alright, but sometimes taste vaguely of an old can. You're an old can!

*Wood Ear- (see above: black fungus)

Replacements for mushrooms: squash, zucchini, tempeh, cooked beans, artichoke hearts, dried tomatoes, dried olives, olives (so many kinds), eggplant, or roasted peppers.

NATTO- This is fermented, slimy-ass soybean. It smells pretty intense/crazy, but if you like pungent flavors, it is good with rice and can be nice in sushi in very small amounts. Replace with- miso, pungent pickle, radish pickle, or fermented black bean sauce

PARSLEY- Italian is the flat-leafed sort and has a milder flavor than curly. Although I am a fan of both. Honestly, celery greens are closer to Italian parsley than curly parsley is in flavor, but you can use them fairly interchangeably here.

PIGEON PEAS- This would be called toor dal at a south Asian/Indian store. Also called "Congo peas." They are tasty and round, without a very combative flavor or texture. Pretty versatile. You might get into them. For the purposes here, get dried and cook them yourself. Canned are just not going to be the same. A Caribbean or West/Central African store is another likely place to find them. Or a bean store (you have those, right?!). Substitute- green lentils, garbanzos or blackeyed peas. Any of them will work.

QUINOA- By now everyone knows quinoa, but you might not be familiar with black or red. Red has a slightly nuttier taste to my palette. The black is tiny and will fall through a lot of strainers even when cooked, so watch it. The black has a fun texture—a bit like chewy poppy seeds. A lot of people wash quinoa before cooking to remove tannins. I usually do, but they bother some people a lot more than others. Some people think quinoa always tastes moldy (that's a thing), whereas for me it's amaranth that always tastes moldy and quinoa is great. To each their own (whiny whining). There is some dispute at the moment about whether quinoa is a seed, or a grain, or what. And also whether it is kosher for Passover or not (generally it's avoided due to guilt by association, in this case). If you are concerned about where it comes from, domestic quinoa is easily available and has been in production since the 80's, so fa-dee-dah! Substitute: red, brown or black rice; millet; buckwheat; kasha; bulghur; and so much more! But not amaranth. That shit is nasty!

ROSEWATER & ORANGE BLOSSOM WATER-

You know I can't remember if these are even used in here, but you could add them to stuff for a little floral pizazz! Rosewater can be strong, and make sure it is in a medium that is edible! Orange Blossom Water is used in Indian cooking and also has a floral-creamsicle flavor. A little of that goes a long way. They can substitute for other floral essences and flavors due to their high availability. Very delicious added to iced teas, ice creams and cakes, lemonade, lassi and other enticing treats and beverages.

SEAWEED-

Your common ones:

*Arame- Also called sea oak, this one is a little sweet and mildly salty, and tends to be in long, thin, scraggly strips. Makes great soup, salad, or pasta substitute. Reconstitutes in about four or five minutes in water.

*Dulse- This one can be added to anything! It's a little purple-y and can be a bit salty, but its character is pretty versatile depending on what you do to it. It reconstitutes in water very quickly—about two minutes.

*Hijiki- When broken up, these look a bit like thin little bat wings. Thus it is fun, and stange, to add it to salads, casseroles, salsas, dips and other such amusing locations. Takes a while to reconstitute in water—about 30 minutes. Taste is pleasant, a little sweet, and pretty oceany. Don't be ascared!

*Irish Moss- You will note that this one is in a lot of strange substances like fake cheese and real cream! It's where carageenan comes from. Doesn't really have tremendous flavor, which is probably why it is used for such pseudo-industrial purposes (clarifying beer as well). You're not going to be using it in here. Just thought I'd share!

*Kombu- This is usually a dark purple and comes in big strips. It's used to flavor broth. You can add it to rice, stews, and soups to flavor them. Has a strong salty "umami" taste, but not fishy. It will expand and soak up water, so you might need to add a cup or two extra of liquid when using it for a broth.

*Nori- This is the one that your sushi rolling sheets are made out of. Makes a great snack and some tasty crisps!

*Spirulina- A lot of ye olde peoples used to make cakes out of this, as it's crap full of nutrients. Esentially, it's a good supplement in small quantities and you can add it to stuff if you like without much consequence. It's easily overwhelmed by other flavors. However, it makes things bright green. It's gonna be in powdered form.

*Wakame- This one is brownish green and tastes great. It takes about ten minutes to reconstitute. Has a good, soft texture when cooked. Good for soups and salads. You will often see this or arame as "seaweed salad" (especially when still a little firm). It expands vastly when reconstituted.

Substitutions for sushi: Rice wrapper, lettuces or chard or other greens, or soy skin.

Substitutions for flavor: Toasted, ground sesame seeds with salt; toasted rice powder; ume plum vinegar; MSG; or strong mushroom broth

SUMAC- This is a very tasty red spice that comes from the berries 'pon yet another shrub (drupes or sumac bobs are the fruits/berries on it). The flavor is slightly citrus, and it is good sprinkled on just about anything. It can be a main ingredient in zahter. If you see a shaker with red stuff in it that isn't chili on your table at a middle eastern place, or it's sprinkled on your dish, it is probably sumac. No it's not poison sumac. That doesn't sound very delicious now, does it!?

TAHINI- This is a paste made out of ground sesame seeds and oil. When combined with salt, garlic and lemon juice, well hey, it suddenly tastes better! A good addition to any salad dressing, sauce, fake cheeze blend, or anything you need to make more delicious. Easy to make in a blender or food processor.

TAMARIND

- This is a brown pod with blackish-purple flesh inhabited by pesky, inedible black seeds and stringy, brown strands. For it to be super fresh, you'd have to peel the husk off, pull out the strands, and cut the seeds out, which is a pain in the ass. Boiling and mashing, and then straining to get the liquid, is a preferred method for tamarind broth, and of course, the drink tamarindo. You can also buy a paste or concentrate, which will be strong. Use a little at a time. It can also come in a block, which will probably still have the seeds in it, that you can boil pieces of to make sauces. Also, there is a drink/soup base that comes in a jar-like thing, which is nothing but tamarind purée. This is prehaps greatest form of all! The taste is rich and sour, with a bit of sweet—sort of like a sour prune, if anything. It jazzes up beverages, curries and stews, soups, and even desserts. Good, very useful stuff. Sometimes it's candied with chili (and often salt), which is pretty damn good. These will often have a seed in them though, just so ya know.

Substitute with: Sour cherry, prunes, jamaica (hibiscus), preserved lemon, etc.

TEMPEH

- This is different than tofu, and to many, has a more appealing texture. Here the soy is bound and fermented in a cake, sometimes with grains, and has a very firm texture compared to tofu. It tastes maybe a little mustier and saltier. It still sucks up flavor much like tofu does and will really take in a marinade. Comes from Indonesia originally.

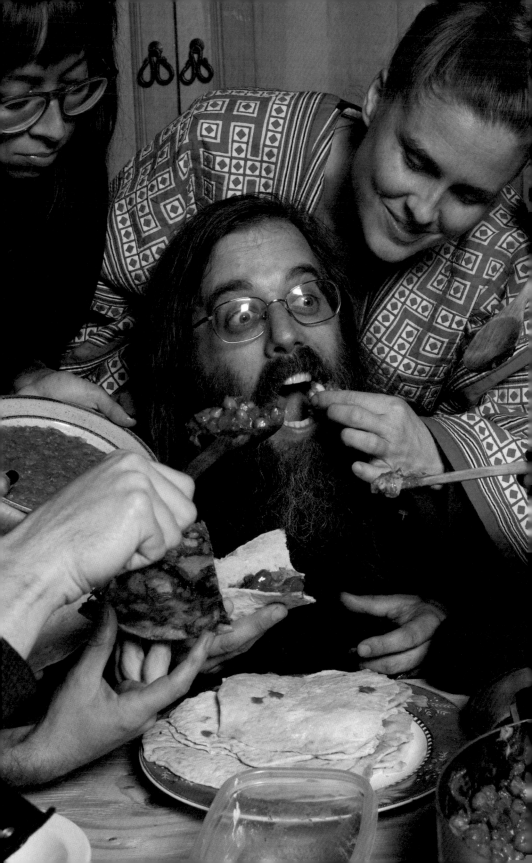

"EAT ME."
- NOEL PONTHIEUX
(INTERNATIONAL CHANTEUSE)

About the AUTHOR
(and contributors)

Joshua Ploeg

(aliases: Joshua Plague, Rocksworth Sexington, Qwerlyn)

Joshua Ploeg has been cooking and languishing in squalor for 15 years. Qualifications include having a secret cafe in his home, cooking for bands, making DIY cookbooks/zines, and half-assedly personal cheffing for room and board. For the past 10 or so years he has toured the country (and the world) cooking for dinner parties and special events in various homes, apartments, warehouses, restaurants, galleries, and venues, while writing food columns for various papers like Satya out of Brooklyn and Sacramento's Midwtown Monthly. A different kitchen and a different crowd every night.

He has played in numerous punk, noise, and newstalgic folk acts for 20+ years. Punk bands he is/was in that no one cares about include: Behead the Prophet No Lord Shall Live, Warm Streams, Mukilteo Fairies, Lords of Lighstpeed, Kiss Me Kill Me, The Special Friend, Sanctuary of Sound, and the most current, Select Sex.

Originally from the Pacific Northwest, he was right there for queercore, riot grrrl and all of that kind of crap, and helped ruin punk for everyone. He has put on shows, housed bands, and lived in cruddy punk houses for most of his life. His punk roots go back to ye olde '80s, when he was introduced through listening to records from his cool uncles, hip mom, and punk/goth sister. In other words, he knows what the fuck he's talking about.

COOKBOOKS:

In Search of the Lost Taste (with artwork by Aaron Renier and Nate Beaty), *So Raw It's Downright Filthy, Fire and Ice, Something Delicious This Way Comes: Spellbinding Vegan Cookery, Dutch Much?, Twelve Knights in My Kingdom, A Typografic Meal to Celebrate the 75th Anniversary of Libelle* (with design and concept by Marc Hollenstein, Steven Serrato and Julie van Severen), *Superfoods series: Cacao* (I offered the recipes for this book as a collaboration with vegan dietician Matt Ruscigno), *Year-Round Vegan Holiday Cooking*, and this title: *This Ain't No Picnic*.

(He also has put out around 30 zines, but those are all hard to find. So punk.)

-Contributors-

Zack Carlson was born in a pizza. He's a hard-working failure in several aspects of the entertainment industry, from screenwriting to film and television production. He has over 4000 VHS tapes and co-authored the book **Destroy All Movies!!!: The Complete Guide to Punks on Film.** He doesn't eat fruit or vegetables.

Eric Ingrate has eaten many a stale dumpster bagel through years of work with Seattle Food Not Bombs, Anarchist Book Fair organizing, and general explorations in trash reclamation. He is a co-editor of **Prisoners' Dilemma** zine, and a frequent contributor to the online Anarchy 101 forum, as well as the book by the same name.

Monica Sklar has a Ph.D. in Design-Apparel Studies focused on socio-cultural, behavioral, and historical aspects of dress. She has taught numerous college level courses in dress and retailing, and published widely on apparel, especially as it relates to subculture. She has also worked in art and design museums/galleries in multiple capacities, done many projects in fashion and art journalism and wardrobe styling, and toiled on countless retail floors. Her book **Punk Style** (Bloomsbury Publishers) features a comprehensive discussion on the subject, including numerous interviews and images, as well her personal insights from decades spent in the scene.

Ilsa Hess is the owner/operator of Love & Joy Foods, makers of Nacheez vegan nacho cheese sauce. Ilsa's lifelong career in computers ended when she was laid off from the County of Sacramento as an IT Analyst. However, she was then finally free to pursue her passion: vegan cooking. She is currently compiling a vegan solar cooking cookbook, as well as finding fun new ways to promote her product, **Nacheez.**

After having decided that he did not suffer sufficiently in punk through his involvement rocking with **Blatz, The Criminals, or The Gr'ups, Jesse Luscious** took the even less glorious positions of volunteering for **The Gilman Street Project,** working for **Lookout Records,** and his present day position as general manager of **Alternative Tentacles.**

Joe Biel was emotionally orphaned to punk rock in Cleveland in 1992. Four years later, he founded **Microcosm Publishing** in a punkhouse, and learned to feed himself by getting hired at an Italian restaurant. 72% of his musical involvement in punk these days is listening to LPs while he makes dinner or does the dishes. The only things he's ever learned to cook well are mashed potatoes (add vegenaise!) and tomato sauce from scratch (patience and pre-planning). He relies on Joshua for most of his decent meals.

Stiff Leggings is a loud, aggravating person about town and a highly shrewd critic of everything everyone else ever did. Played the harpoonica in the **Shitty Bastards** and **Noise Annoyze.**

Dalton Blanco is a photographer, videographer, and musician living in California. When he's not eating deep fried ice cream, he's eating deep fried bananas.

Vice Cooler writes and photographs for **Rolling Stone, Vice Magazine;** and **photographs for ANP quarterly, i-D Magazine, The Wire,** and **San Francisco Bay Guardian.** He is the singer and songwriter for **Hawnay Troof** and **Xbxrx.** He was crowned by **Peaches** as the world's greatest performer. **High Places** and **Henry Rollins** have referred to him as an "inspiration."

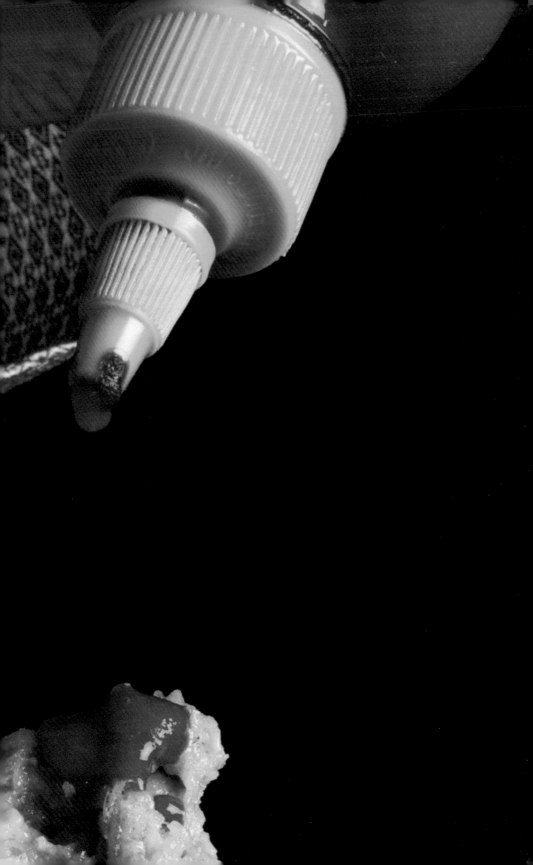

IDEAS FOR MENUS

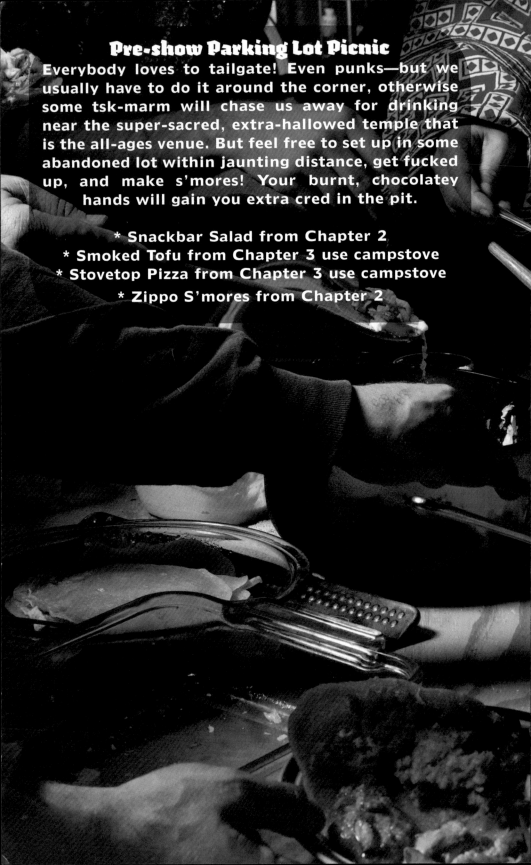

Pre-show Parking Lot Picnic

Everybody loves to tailgate! Even punks—but we usually have to do it around the corner, otherwise some tsk-marm will chase us away for drinking near the super-sacred, extra-hallowed temple that is the all-ages venue. But feel free to set up in some abandoned lot within jaunting distance, get fucked up, and make s'mores! Your burnt, chocolatey hands will gain you extra cred in the pit.

* Snackbar Salad from Chapter 2
* Smoked Tofu from Chapter 3 use campstove
* Stovetop Pizza from Chapter 3 use campstove
* Zippo S'mores from Chapter 2

Takeout for the Road

Many punks are overgrown adolescents, so feel free to play mommy or daddy and make some fabulous to-go meals for those boys, girls, and the rest heading out on a long long, long trip. Just pack some nuts, raisins, and chickosticks for the little buggers in their Exploited lunchbox and send them on their way! If they don't eat, they get pissed off. It makes for better songs, but might cause them to break up before they get to the show.

* Safety Orange Delite from Chapter 5
* Giant Stuffed Biscuit from Chapter 7 biscuit travels well
* Coffee Pot Curry from Chapter 2
* Donuts from Chapter 1, love ya mom!!

Absorbent Meal for a Hard Night of Drinkin'

When you have guzzled five 40's of Cobra you need a lil' help to keep your woozy gut in check, especially something that will soak up some of the alcohol, so you don't pass out before the show. With this chic menu you may even be able to get a fifth down as well. And it will create a dumpling in your stomach that you can have surgically removed and feast on again later!

* Anarchy Burger and Crisps both from Chapter 1, so you can drunkenly scream "Anarchyburger" over and over for an hour or two.
* Burrito from Chapter 8 *(It's really a chimichanga, remember, and who doesn't like late night fried shit?! Drunk or no!)*
* Any of the flour-based stuff from Chapter 3
* Bagel Bread Pudding from Chapter 6

First Date

AKA Last Date: Dress to impress and only make the best! These will ensure you're in for a good night of food fun! We're here to help...You won't even realize you are on a date! Which is great, because slobber is not vegan.

* Actual Deconstructed Sushi from Chapter 5
* Chickn Vindaloo from Chapter 1, and then "I Just Wanna Have Something to Do" will become your song. And after you break up, you can cry whenever you hear The Ramones and demand the song be turned off, in order to accommodate your own personal comfort level, whenever it plays in a public space.
* Zucchini Bread from Chapter 8, Dainty doings for your dainty moves.
* Beer Caramel Popcorn from Chapter 6, For your special movie enjoyment afterwards, where you can get each other sticky.

You know I had once been working on a zine of advice on how to impress potential woo-ees which including fashion and lighting tips, menus, and recipes, conversation suggestions, and dance moves. It was entitled *A Cornucopia of Advanced Weaponry*, but I never finished it. I would never follow my own advice anyway. I'm too much of a slob.

Dinner Party For The Socially Awkward

This is like first date, but more realistic. Here the food can easily take the place of any dull conversation. Awkwardness in emo-punk climates is exalted to the point of superhero status. The more plaintive and hapless, the better. However, those types might not make for a very exciting gathering. Simply make and consume, and voila! Your mouth will be full of something the whole night!

* **Dashboard Jerky** from chapter 2, because explaining what you did, and everyone *almost* excitedly talking about it, should take up at least 20 minutes. This is your best chance to liven the mood, as if that's going to happen...
* **Flashy Trio of Dips** from Chapter 4. You may be amused when your guests accidentally get these on their favorite sweater. And cry und cry.
* **Tomatoes Four Ways** from Chapter 7 and **Stovetop Cornbread** from Chapter 3. Be Thrilled as you are regaled with dead silence because no one knows who **Tomata du Plenty** is.
* **Fishnet Tarts** from Chapter 4. Except pay attention and do it right, unlike the photo! The potentially inappropriate sexuality of fishnets ought to chase everyone away, then you won't have to just go in your room and wait for them to leave on their own like you did last time.

Eating Dinner Alone

Let's face it, you will be alone for most of your life. So we present dinner for one! For those who hate Valentine's Day because you have no one! Single and resentin' it!

* **Emo Lemon Drop** from Chapter 5, Because you drink alone with nobody else when you're cryyyyy'yyyin!
* **Rip Her to Shreds** from Chapter 7, Because you are very angry, and want to be alone, and kill everyone, yet maintain your supple figure *(just in case somebody hot knocks on the door).*
* **Bloodstains** from Chapter 4, Because you are still very, very angry
* **Pop punk Cupcakes** from Chapter 5, Cuz... you're... so... happyhappyhappyhappyhappyhappy

Holidays

A generic spectacular meal plan to WOW! for any holiday. Thrill at the magic loaftiplying* morsels as we present for your holy ceremony the most decadent platters of enjoyment to fulfill your jubilent cavalcade!

I just made that word up, it means "to magically create abundance."

* Leopard Mezza from Chapter 4. Let the fun-citement begin!
* Baked Squash from Chapter 6. Because it might be cheap and you can always find a squash!
* Tidy Henry from Chapter 7. Because you need some big ol' sloppy thing to represent a cornucopia somehow!
* Beer and Uncheez Soup with Bagel Croutons from Chapter 6, Because nothing warms the cockles quite like something made out of a bunch of leftover, stale, and dumpstered crap. Also, this will be a crowd pleaser. And you do want people to be happy, right? I mean, you don't hate joy and comfort and tidings, do you? You do like myrrh and frankincense, don't you? I mean who doesn't, besides baby eaters and puppy killers, amiright?!
* Milkshake from Chapter 7. Now hear me out on this one, people! Add whiskey or vodka and some nutmeg and this is your goddamn eggnog right here! It is also the traditional drink of July 4th.
* And all the while, burn some myrrh. Whatever the F that is!

A Chaotic Dinner That Will Totally Fail!

Expected to cook for everyone because it's your night, but you don't want to? Try this on for size and teach 'em a lesson. They'll cry und cry and write a zine about it.

Trois Plats
* Deconstructed Sushi Haunted House from Chapter 5
and if anyone remains...
* Exploding Hot Dog Surprise from Chapter 7
* Coffee Sludge Jel from Chapter 5

al-hoa
860 n. hill st.

GET OFF THE
CROSS, THE
WOOD IS NEEDED

Zombie Apocalypse Grocery Store Hideout Cookout

Do ya wanna party? It's Party Time!
The delicious smells might attract the zombies, so you will need the **Durian** to make a stench to cover your scent.
Also, make sure you are all hungover, so that you can moan and groan a lot like a bunch of zombies. Have as many true-damn, dirty crusties on junk there as possible, so that there will be plenty of poop, dirt, torn clothes, sunken eyes, and bruises to keep incognito amongst the undead. Enjoy, and burn this fracking system dowwwwwwwn!!

* Snackbar Salad from Chapter 2, Again, but without any fresh fruit
* Durian Soup from Chapter 5, To create the smell of dead bodeee
* Crusty Cupboard Surprise from Chapter 6, Use a campstove
* Chop Suey from Chapter 1, But with all canned shit instead of fresh, and chow mein noodles instead of rice!

Shitty Bastard Brunch

I know, I know—punks **DO NOT** wake up early enough to have brunch technically, but like everyone else, they love brunch. So you can have this meal on punk time, about three hours after it was supposed to start. Just make half the food you were planning and get twice as many people as you invited. Have some bands play, preferrably book three or four, but make sure it winds up being more like eight or nine bands that all share members and sound the same. And who's bringing the PA?! I don't know, I thought you were, man!

* Kir Royale from Chapter 7. To get things started and give some semblance of frippery, which any brunch should maintain.
* 40 oz. Mimosa from Chapter 6. Because now you are really late bringing the food out and this ought to keep them occupied.
* Tofu Scramble from Chapter 8. The reimagined presentation will greatly annoy everyone present.
* Bagel Rarebit from Chapter 6. That ol' brunch classic of yore. I think rich people invented this dish.
* Bagel French Toast from Chapter 6, You can never have enough bagels and you can never have enough toast. If you use blueberry, the smell will entice everyone out of their garbage heap a little earlier, and they will stagger into the kitchen to stand right behind you and scratch themselves muttering "oh, is that for everyone? ...cool."

Another great idea for such entertaining is to have your guests each bring a bag of their favorite dumpstered bagel, then you are certain to have enough for the whole neighborhood!

INDEX